MELIZ BERG

DINNER TONIGHT

MELIZ BERG

DINNER TONIGHT

SIMPLE MEALS FULL OF MEDITERRANEAN FLAVOR

Interlink Books

an imprint of Interlink Publishing Group, Inc.
Northampton, Massachusetts

Contents

Introduction

"Ok, what are we having for dinner tonight?" is genuinely a question I ask myself every day, even as a food writer—in fact, it's a phrase most of us use on the daily. I'm a creature of habit, a mom of two. I need simple cooking most days, which can mean a few different things to me depending on what I've got going on. On some days, I need recipes with minimal prep and cooking times, meals that can be on the table quickly. These are usually reliable family favorites, enhanced with flavorful combinations of my trusty pantry spices, that can be easily cooked in the oven in one pan, or on the stovetop in a single pot. However, even when I'm at home, but have a million things to do, or I just want to take it easy with my family, I need the simplicity of recipes with short preparation times that I can put in the oven and not worry about.

Although I cannot forgo the deliciousness of the traditional Turkish-Cypriot dishes I have grown up with, some of my family recipes can certainly be a labor of love. When I have the time, I adore the process that goes into making dishes such as *dolma* (rolled and stuffed vine leaves and vegetables) and anything dough based; but the reality is, I don't always have the time. Consequently, I have adjusted some of the processes and ingredients a little to suit my daily lifestyle, without ever compromising the true essence of the recipes in question. To give me the flavors I crave, I've created easier, shortcut versions of some of my most beloved family recipes, or have given them a little twist with a slight change in method or ingredients.

A FRUGAL WAY TO EAT

It is from these traditional Turkish-Cypriot dishes that I have learned so much from cooking with my mom. She is so relaxed and calm in the kitchen (I am still working on this), goes with the flow, and uses whatever she has on hand. With one arm maneuvering a piece of fabric under the sewing machine, and another preparing dinner, I watched my mom multitask her days like a pro when we were younger. Working from home (or in her brother's clothing factory in Tottenham, London), while running an unforgiving, yet devoted, taxi-service for me and my siblings, we were so lucky to know that she would always ensure there was a family dinner on the table each and every night, even if they were made up of bulked-up leftovers from the days before.

I've learned to never waste a scrap from the fridge, ideas for which I regularly share on my online social platforms, and to batch-cook meals that are portioned off to last a few days, or be frozen. Leftovers were always concocted into something new the following night, such as using leftover mash to make ground meat go further, like my mom's Mash-Topped Meat *Börek* (page 165). We'd have the pies with canned boiled potatoes, peas and gravy. The addition of the mashed potatoes, canned vegetables and a hot, meaty pouring sauce my mom had never even seen or heard of for the first 20 years of her life was a clear reflection of the food customs she had absorbed since moving to the UK. Marrying these food customs with the traditional methods she'd use to make these delicious things was an homage to our diasporic Turkish-Cypriot existence. My childhood food traditions have undoubtedly shaped the way I now cook for my own family.

Many of the recipes have frugality at the core, and my deep-rooted objection to waste food has been ingrained in me since birth. Every carrot, celery stick and onion is used up in a soup or stew, or finely diced and stored in freezer-bag batches ready to add to recipes whenever I require them. Finely chopping up any sad-looking vegetables and storing them in the freezer also saves a lot of preparation time. Freeze ready-to-use portions of finely chopped carrots, celery and onions on a shallow baking pan first to prevent them from sticking together, and then evenly distribute the vegetables into reusable freezer bags. I always turn to the freezer when making *Ezogelin* Soup (page 52) and the one-pot Creamy *Hellim* & Tomato Orzo (page 60).

The recipes here are my go-to inspiration day in, day out, and the dishes I have been told people would love to have handy in a cookbook in their own kitchens.

Aside from making the most out of what we had, there were always a few key, budget-friendly salad ingredients and fresh herbs in the fridge, and certainly a few blocks of *hellim* (halloumi cheese) ready to make into a quick light-bite. We'd throw pasta straight into sauces rather than boiling it first and make soups and stews from whatever dried grains, herbs and condiments were preserved and stocked in the pantry. This style of cooking is not only satisfying and creative, but it also equips you with the simple skills to cook something delicious, even with just a small number of ingredients.

I always cook down vegetables in olive oil, and salad dressings are never made without excellent quality, rich extra virgin olive oil. My fridge is regularly stocked with fresh carrots, celery and lemons, and herbs such as parsley and cilantro, which can all be frozen to save on prep-time. Freshly squeezed lemon juice and finely chopped parsley can be frozen in ice cube trays—just top up the finely chopped herbs with a little cold water so they are easier to pop out and into recipes, such as hot soups and stews.

QUICK AND SATISFYING

If there is one thing that gives me a lot of satisfaction in the kitchen (especially when I'm hungry or on-the-go), it's creating something packed full of flavor, really rather quickly. Over the years I've developed a repertoire of "fast and fresh" recipes that can be on the table in a matter of minutes, to swiftly satisfy impatient appetites or a busy lifestyle.

COOK NOW TO EAT LATER

I really wanted this book to showcase the variety of simple, mouthwatering meals that can be made from accessible, flavorful ingredients and prepped for the week ahead. There are recipes where the flavors improve over time, such as the Green Bean Stew (page 79) or Pea & Ground Lamb Stew (page 80) stored in the fridge to be eaten over the next couple of days, or recipes which can be made then divided up into lunch boxes, such as the Loaded Pasta, Grain or Rice Salad (page 40), and recipes to be made then frozen for when you need them, such as White Cheese & Spinach Open-Faced *Börek* (page 26).

A NOTE ON AIR FRYING AND SLOW COOKING

I love a reliable one-pan bake and an all-in-one-pot meal, and I cook them using traditional methods on the stovetop and in the oven. However, I've also included different cooking options where I think they work well, so you can choose what suits you better. I have found that all slow cookers and air fryers do vary, so timings may need to be adjusted slightly depending on the size of your machine. If your air fryer has a double-basket, then you can cook two batches at once; if not, then you may have to cook some of the recipes in two batches (such as the Crispy Chicken Wings on page 106) to guarantee the best results. You'll find all my tips on adjusting the recipes for slow cookers and air fryers on page 199. I've included air fryer and slow cooker methods for a handful of the recipes to give you an idea of how I'd adjust them to suit these appliances. If you are already handy using either/both of them, then feel free to play around with the recipes you feel confident would also work in this way.

COOKING FOR EVERYONE'S NEEDS

Gluten-free: My father-in-law follows a strict gluten-free diet and, for the past decade or so, I have made a conscious effort to make gluten-free versions of the recipes we all love to eat as a family. I've given instructions on how to make the recipes gluten free (there are only five recipes in the book where this isn't possible, unless you can get your hands on gluten-free orzo or know how to make or source good-quality gluten-free filo, then it's only three!), with a separate gluten-free pastry recipe for my mom's Mash-Topped Meat *Börek* (page 165) and *Hellimli* Yorkshire Puddings (page 193). For any pasta-based recipes, I swap in gluten-free pasta; I check the pasta 3–5 minutes ahead of the cooking time in my recipes, depending on what the packet instructions suggest, because the pasta can get mushy and break apart very easily if you overcook it even for a couple of minutes.

Plant-based: I'm getting asked more and more about whether or not my recipes can be made plant-based, and the majority of the ones in this book certainly can, bar a few obvious fish and meaty ones. For recipes that call for ground meat or dairy products such as milk, butter, yogurt, cream and cheese, feel free to substitute these for your favorite plant-based alternatives. When making the *köfte* (patty or meatball) recipes, I suggest mixing together 1 tablespoon of flaxseed meal or milled flaxseed (golden or brown is fine) with 2 tablespoons of cold water as an egg replacement. Leave the liquid flaxseed mixture to stand for 5 minutes, stir well, then mix it into the rest of the ingredients in the recipe to help bind and shape the *köfte*.

STAYING IN WITHOUT MISSING OUT

The "Friday night fakeout" has certainly become a fun addition to our weekly family menu and I have gained so much joy from seeing others replicate our family fake-takeout dinners at home. I have included my tried-and-tested favorites, and have also given suggestions for what to group them with, for a slightly more extravagant spread everyone can share.

The weekend is our family's time to cook together, to take it slower, or to ramp up the action (without too much fuss) when and if entertaining is on the radar. I am a bit of a perfectionist, and historically, having guests over would be something I'd fret about or do too much for; the feeling that I always had to impress would override the genuine pleasure I'd gain from cooking and spending time with my friends and family. Over the years, I have had to remind myself that guests come over to see you, to spend time with you, and not to see you running around like a headless chicken. So here you'll find my trusted recipes for cooking for others—no headless chickens included!

All the recipes are packed full of flavor, but can be prepared in advance (and stored in the fridge), or made extremely quickly, to be thrown in the oven to do their thing, perhaps with a simple garnish at the end (you can get your guests to help you with that bit unless you struggle to delegate, like *moi*).

When it comes to baking, I rely on my favorite bread recipes and sweet treats time and time again. I have added flavorful twists to some of my best-loved cakes and bakes, such as flipping over a traditional crumble and infusing it with the flavors of a nutty, spiced *baklava* (page 185), and taking the ingredients in traditional (and rather lengthy to make) Cypriot breads and pastries such as *Hellimli* (Halloumi Bread) and *Pilavuna* and turning them into quick and easy muffins, loaves (page 191) and even Yorkshire Puddings (page 193).

You may find yourself having a meatless weekend, cooking a one-pot meal on a Monday, and favoring a fakeout on a Thursday, so feel free to play around with what suits you as and when—variety is the spice of life, after all.

NEVER COMPROMISE ON FLAVOR

When I'm craving particular flavors but want to keep the cooking simple, I like to reach for the essential ingredients only. I might not have much time but I refuse to compromise on flavor. Some of the ingredients lists in this book might look long, but you'll find that most of them are just a concoction of the same essentials from the fridge and pantry that I regularly use, and have recommended on pages 15–21. The same spices, stock cubes and pastes feature throughout, to ensure that you always have exactly what you need to make something delicious.

From training and working as a secondary school music teacher to starting off a recipe blog on a bit of a whim, it makes me so proud to see that the wholesome and achievable recipes I share online, and from my first book, *Meliz's Kitchen*, have now become staple meals in countless households across the world. I hope *Dinner Tonight* will provide you with a plentiful selection of simple, yet exciting recipes that you can rely on every day of the week.

WHAT RECIPE WHEN?

Throughout the book, I've included one of the notes below alongside each recipe. You can immediately see what you'll be getting from the cooking experience, allowing you to choose the recipe(s) that suit(s) your situation best:

FAST AND FILLING:
The entire prep and cooking time is typically 30 minutes or less.

FAST AND FRESH:
Also typically 30 minutes or less from start to finish. These are the sort of recipes I crave on a warmer day, when I want something delicious but a bit lighter, like a salad.

ALL IN ONE:
All the ingredients go into one pot or pan to cook with less dish washing!

QUICK PREP, SLOW COOK:
The prep time is 15 minutes or less and then you can put the dish into the oven (or onto the stove, or into the slow cooker or air fryer) to cook away happily until you're ready to eat.

TRADITIONAL RECIPE, CHEATER'S VERSION:
Those treasured family recipes with shortcut methods.

TRADITIONAL FLAVORS, NEW RECIPE:
These are the dishes inspired by some of my all-time-favorite family recipes, but I've married the flavors with new methods and ingredients.

Turn to page 214 for an additional index of categorized recipes.

Essential Ingredients for Maximum Flavor

There are a number of ingredients I use throughout the book that bring so much flavor to a meal and are fundamental to the way I cook. My pantry is never without spices and herbs such as *pul biber* (Aleppo pepper/Turkish red pepper flakes), dried mint and cumin, and condiments such as *tatlı biber salçası* (Turkish sweet/mild red pepper paste), pomegranate molasses and olive oil, which are used to enrich sauces and marinades. I advise you to keep these ingredients in your kitchens to whip up something exciting and delicious with.

Most of the ingredients can be found in mainstream supermarkets, and I have taken the time to explain a few in a little more detail.

Pul Biber (Aleppo Pepper/Turkish Red Pepper Flakes)

Pul biber, also known as Aleppo pepper or Turkish red pepper flakes, are oilier, warmer, tangier, fruitier, finer and perhaps a little saltier than the standard chile flakes you'll find in your local supermarket. I sprinkle them onto things, season with and add them to marinades, sauces and dressings. If you struggle to find *pul biber*, look for Aleppo pepper flakes, which are essentially the same. Do note that I use the regular-sized flakes instead of the *ipek* (finer) flakes, but either will suffice.

Extra Virgin Olive Oil

The intensity of a good extra virgin olive oil makes such a difference to the flavor and quality of salad dressings and mezze dishes, so it's a good idea to keep stocked up with the stuff. Obviously, being biased, I naturally favor Cypriot extra virgin olive oil. Due to the intensity of its richer, fuller-bodied flavor (and color), I reserve the use of extra virgin olive oil for luscious salad dressings, sauces and to drizzle over finished dishes, but occasionally cook with it too.

Olive Oil

Whether I'm softening, frying, brushing or baking ingredients, my choice of oil to cook with will always be olive oil. Most of my savory recipes include olive oil, and the cake recipes in this book are all made with olive oil, so do ensure to keep a large bottle of it in your pantry. As a general rule, I mostly use olive oil when cooking on the stove, in the oven or in marinades.

Cinnamon (ground and stick/bark)

Cypriots love cinnamon; in tea, ground meat-based recipes, pasta dishes, with honey, roasted in slow-cooked roasts and stews, in cakes, breads and syrups. We use it in abundance, so keep yourselves stocked up with both ground cinnamon and sticks/bark.

Cumin

The earthy counterpart to cinnamon, I use cumin to flavor *köfte* (meatballs and patties) recipes and to add some umami to both meat and vegetable-based stews.

Tatlı Biber Salçası (Turkish Sweet/Mild Red Pepper Paste)

There are two varieties of *biber salçası* (red pepper paste)—*tatlı* (sweet/mild) and *acı* (hot). I prefer to use the *tatlı* (sweet/mild) variety in order to be able to control the amount of spice and heat I put in. Once opened, ensure you store the *salça* in the fridge—flatten down the top of the paste and drizzle over a little olive oil to prevent it from spoiling. I also freeze portions in ice cube trays ready to use in marinades, sauces and stews—it is wonderful added into a ragù or *bolonez* (Bolognese) sauce.

Pomegranate Molasses

I use this to add a sweet, rich tartness to marinades, sauces and salad dressings. Try to source the best pomegranate molasses you can find/afford, for the quality that comes from purely natural ingredients and a concentrated depth of flavor.

Black Olives

I rarely cook with pitted olives, and instead prefer to buy whole dry black olives that I pit myself before using; I find that the olives retain their texture and moisture better this way. Cypriot black olives are softer and pinker inside than dry black olives, but they're drier and more wrinkly than Kalamata olives (due to being brined and then cured with salt). However, if I don't have Cypriot black olives on hand, I use small, dry black Turkish olives or meaty Kalamata ones.

Yufka (Filo Pastry)

Filo pastry comes in so many varieties, and the recipe for *Yufka Mantısı* on page 145 calls for sheets of traditional Turkish *yufka* (usually homemade), which are just slightly thicker than the filo sheets you can find in mainstream supermarkets to make *baklava* or *börek* (filled pastries) with. However, if you

can't source Turkish *yufka* (Turkish/International supermarkets sell it), then double up two large, good quality sheets of store-bought filo instead. The same can be said for the Tahini Helva Stuffed Filo Rolls on page 175—if you can't find the smaller, thicker, triangular-shaped filo sheets known as *üçgen yufka* from your local Turkish or international supermarkets (they are pretty easy to source), then fold over a thin sheet of filo and cut it into a triangle—the texture of the finished *börek* will differ just slightly, but it will still be delicious.

Middle Eastern/Persian/Lebanese Cucumbers

My dad would always buy us these small cucumbers from the international supermarket; they are around half the size, in width and thickness, of a small English cucumber. Some are straight, some are curly, but as a general rule they are all crispier and sweeter than their Western counterparts, and the seeds are much smaller. They are also more flavorful and less likely to water down dishes, so I always use them in salads and dips. My favorite cucumbers when I was a child were pickling cucumbers called crooks; they are curly and quite thin, the skin has pronounced ridges, and they are not watery at all. They are utter gold in a salad, or simply sliced in half and sprinkled with salt—my favorite childhood snack.

Sesame Seeds

Pretty much every baked *börek*, bread and savory cake I grew up eating was sprinkled with sesame seeds, often accompanied by its favorite partners in crime for Cypriot baked goods, *garacocco/çörek otu* (nigella seeds) and *anason* (aniseed). To enrich their nutty flavor, I toast sesame seeds when sprinkling them over mezze dishes and dips; just ensure you keep stirring while toasting in a pan so that they color evenly and don't burn.

Tahini (Sesame Seed Paste)

Sesame seeds are also the essential ingredient in tahini, where the seeds are ground into a thick, yet runny, paste. I opt for excellent-quality smooth, nutty and creamy varieties of tahini to whip into sauces and dips. The quality of the ingredients here will make such a difference to the outcome of the finished dish.

Dried Mint

Mint is fundamental in Cypriot, and some Turkish, savory recipes, and I use it in abundance, usually in its dried form; in *köfte* (meatballs and patties), *dolma* (stuffed leaves and vegetables), pasta dishes, pastries and salad dressings. Mainstream supermarket mint (fresh and dried) is darker in color and not as light or sweet as Cypriot mint. I always opt for Cypriot or Turkish-branded varieties of the dried herb, which are akin to the softer scent and flavor of the mint grown in Cyprus. You could also dry your own fresh mint leaves: remove the leaves from the stalks, wash and dry the leaves thoroughly, then lay them out on a clean tea towel or double-layered paper towels, in an area in your kitchen which sees the sun (it's best to do this in the summer, when the temperature is hotter). After a few days, once the leaves have started to shrivel and turn darker in color, you should be able to crush them between your fingers. If the leaves don't crumble easily, then leave them for another day or so. Once fully dried, keep them in an airtight container and crumble into or over recipes where required.

Coarse Black Pepper & Sea Salt Flakes

You'll see in most of my recipes that I opt for coarse black pepper and sea salt flakes (fine sea salt too) in place of ground black pepper or table salt. I find that it's much easier to control the seasoning of recipes when using coarse black pepper and flaky (and fine) sea salt, as the finer consistency of ground black pepper and table salt can be intensely overpowering, ruining a dish entirely if you accidentally put in a little too much. Fine sea salt is subtle in flavor, especially when seasoning slow-cooked soups and stews, and I also use sea salt flakes and coarse black pepper for garnishing and seasoning dishes with just before serving.

Fresh Lemons

Ensure to keep your fridges stocked up with lemons for my recipes, as they are an essential ingredient in salad dressings and for adding to soups and stews. I freeze freshly squeezed lemon juice in ice cube trays and just pop out the cubes and into hot soups and stews to save on time and washing up, and to prevent food waste. You can also freeze lemon zest.

Beyaz Peynir (Turkish White Cheese)

Chopped, crumbled, sliced or placed into baked goods and börek (pastries), beyaz peynir (white cheese) comes in many different types and varieties. Ezine Peynir, from Ezine in Çanakkale, is my favorite Turkish white cheese, and if you can source it, then please do use it; it is rich and creamy. If you're struggling to get your hands on Turkish white cheese, then you could use feta.

Sumac

In Turkish-Cypriot cuisine, summak (sumac) is used more as a garnish for salads and mezze dishes rather than a spice used to flavor cooked recipes, although I do use it to add a zing to the Spiced Roasted Cauliflower, Potatoes & Chickpeas (page 64). Sumac, as a spice, is made from ground dried sumac berries and is quite tangy in flavor, adding natural lemony notes to salads, such as the onion, parsley and sumac salad used to top the Cheater's *Lahmacun* Pitas (page 105).

Yogurt

A pot of thick, preferably strained, plain yogurt is a fridge-staple. Strained yogurt is known as *süzme yoğurt* in Turkish; a large dollop can be eaten as a simple side to any stewed meal, it can be used as a meat-tenderizer in marinades, or whipped into bread-dunking-worthy mezze dips. It is a beautiful addition in achieving a soft and luscious texture to cakes, and can be strained for a few hours to create a thicker, light cream cheese-like consistency which can then be used as an alternative to cream and frosting.

Fresh Parsley & Cilantro

Köfte (meatball and patty) recipes are seldom made without finely chopped flat leaf parsley, and a large portion of my dishes are garnished with a sprinkling of this fresh, unimposing herb. Traditional Cypriot salads that are customarily made with cilantro can be substituted for parsley if you have an aversion for the former, but do not be tempted to substitute fresh parsley for fresh cilantro in cooked recipes; the finished dish will taste completely different to its intended flavor profile.

Hellim

Hellim is the Turkish-Cypriot word (and halloumi the Greek-Cypriot word) for the cheese unique to the island of Cyprus and synonymous with its cuisine. *Hellim* is traditionally made with raw (unpasteurized), unhomogenized sheep (ewe) and/or goat milk, and rennet, which helps to thicken and bring the curds together, separating them from the whey (which is used to make ricotta). *Hellim* isn't traditionally "squeaky"; in its truest form, it's hot and creamy when freshly made, and should be semi-hard once brined in salty water, which helps preserve it. Cow milk is often added to less-traditional *hellim*, to aid mass-production or if finding enough seasonal sheep and goat milks gets tricky. The cow's milk adds a higher-lactose content to the *hellim* as well as a squeakier texture, so always opt for the more traditional sheep and goat *hellim* if you can. I use *hellim* in everything, like most Cypriots, to add texture, seasoning and comfort to our favorite family dishes; finely grated over pasta, cubed or sliced and fried in olive oil, or as fillings and toppings for sandwiches, breads and pastries. The list is endless, so do ensure to have a block (or six) in your fridge (or freezer, because it can be frozen for up to a year and defrosted in the fridge overnight when needed).

LIGHT BITES
& SNACKS

These are my go-to breakfast, lunch and quick-fix recipes. Here you'll find ideas for jazzing up modest slices of toast and pre-made pastry, as well as flavor-packed salads and satisfying sandwiches that can be made quickly, in advance, packed into lunchboxes, and eaten on the go.

My two favorite versions of grilled cheese are in this chapter, and both can be whipped up in under 30 minutes (page 30 and page 32), although neither of them are made with Cheddar cheese. Since it's no secret that I would happily eat a typical *Kıbrıslı* (Cypriot) breakfast every day for the rest of my life, I've created a speedy, cheesy Cypriot Breakfast *Gabira* (grilled bread/toast) recipe that brings those familiar flavors and ingredients together in a single bite (page 32).

The topping for the Crispy Veggie & Mashed Avocado White Cheese on Toast (page 30) can be made ahead of time. The avocado and white cheese can be smashed and made two days in advance (as the lemon juice will prevent the avocado from turning brown), and if you're not bothered about serving the sautéed vegetables hot, then you can cook up a double batch and store them in the fridge for the following couple of days. If possible, try and source some fresh spearmint or Moroccan mint leaves rather than garden mint, as they really will add a beautiful sweetness to the dish.

Nearly everything in this chapter takes less than 30 minutes to make except for my White Cheese & Spinach Open-Faced *Börek* (page 26) and *Hellim* & Sweet Potato Egg Muffins (page 36), which are my modern takes on two traditional Turkish baked goods. Using ready-rolled puff pastry to whip up the *börek* (filled pastries) cuts down the prepping and

rolling time, before the pastries are oven baked. The muffins have all the flavor of fried *mücver* in an easily transportable baked version—and are so quick to prepare.

This is a chapter where I celebrate the versatility of the humble egg. When I was a secondary school music teacher, one of my quick-and-easy meals after a long day was anything egg based. I knew that if I had a small selection of vegetables in the fridge, a few eggs and a bit of leftover cheese, I could make something delicious and nutritious in no time at all. Since I now predominantly work from home, after taking a hiatus from teaching, I like to keep my fridge and pantry stocked up with ingredients I can put together quickly during breaks in my working day, such as the Whipped Tahini, Spiced Butter & Boiled Egg Salad (page 34).

Please play around with whatever green vegetables and cheese you have for the *Hellim* & Sautéed Vegetable Frittata (page 29), although I would say the contrast of the soft *hellim* cubes within the frittata and the crispy, caramelized grated *hellim* top will always be my preferred choice. I use brown rice, white rice and wild rice, whatever I've got on hand, in the "Throw It All In" Egg-Fried Rice (page 42).

I am a firm believer that if you are going to serve a salad as the main event, then it needs to be loaded—loaded with flavor, goodness and texture. The Cannellini Bean, Crispy *Hellim* & Crunchy Walnut Salad (page 39) delivers all three. Two of my favorite traditional salads are a Turkish-Cypriot *Kuru Fasulye Salatası* (a cannellini bean salad, similar to the Turkish equivalent known as *Piyaz)* and a crunchy *Gavurdağı Salatası. Gavurdağı* originates from the

Gaziantep region in Türkiye, and due to the proximity of the south-eastern part of the country to *Kıbrıs* (Cyprus), this salad, along with many other dishes and influences from *Antepli* cuisine, can also be found in Turkish-Cypriot restaurants and households on the island. The signature traits of a typical *Gavurdağı* are crunchy walnuts, onions, tomatoes, parsley and a simple pomegranate molasses and extra virgin olive oil dressing. I've combined my favorite elements of both salads, as well as chucking in two of my favorite Cypriot ingredients, *hellim* (halloumi cheese) and fresh cilantro, to create this dreamy, loaded, nutritious salad.

Adding hot rice, grains or pasta to a salad allows the flavors in the dressing to really get into those grains. You can make the Loaded Pasta, Grain or Rice Salad (page 40) in advance using hot, cooked microwaveable brown rice or quinoa for ease, if you like. It's a great one for batch cooking, to provide you with a few, pre-prepared lunches throughout the week.

There are a couple of recommendations I have for prepping and storing the salad in advance to save time:

○ Make the salad (minus the avocado and rice) and dressing in advance but do not pour the dressing over the salad. Store the salad and the dressing separately in the fridge for up to three days, and add the appropriate portions of avocado, steaming hot rice and dressing when you are ready to eat it.

○ Make the salad in full, including the steaming-hot rice and eat immediately. Store leftovers in the fridge and only eat fridge-cold for up to three days.

Throughout the book I've played around with many traditional dishes to make them a little quicker and easier to put together, without ever compromising on flavor, and the two sandwich recipes in this chapter are a fine example of this.

Balık Ekmek (literally translated as "fish bread"), a popular street food found typically in the Eminönü area of Istanbul, Türkiye, overlooking the water of the Golden Horn Estuary by the Galata Bridge, is traditionally made with fresh mackerel. The fish is taken straight off the boats, then cooked over hot coals, before being placed into fresh sandwich baguettes or *Somun Ekmeği* (a non-seeded version of the Simple Seeded Loaves on page 191) with an array of salad vegetables.

Although *marul* (long leaf lettuce such as romaine) is the most prevalently used green in the baguettes, I like to use peppery arugula in my *Balık Ekmek*-Style Smoked Mackerel Baguettes (page 45), which gives a lovely contrast to the sweet peppers, tangy tomatoes and pomegranate molasses. Something that cannot be substituted however, are thinly sliced crunchy onions and lemon juice; they are an absolute must. Traditionally, *Balık Ekmek* is often served with a yogurt sauce, which I've swapped for a slightly sweeter, peppery, zesty, minty mayonnaise.

The Seafood Cocktail Pita Pockets (page 46) take 10 minutes to put together and are loaded with crunch and tang from the mixture of cucumbers, radishes, *pul biber* and pomegranate molasses, while still oozing the comforting familiarity that comes from a traditional Shrimp Cocktail. I love loading this filling onto a baked potato or into cooked pasta, as much as I do packing it into a pita.

Whether I'm making my own dough or working with pre-made filo pastry, I do find that I have to set aside a substantial chunk of time to make one of my favorite snacks, savory **beyaz peynirli ıspanaklı** *(white cheese and spinach)* **börek.** *Cue these quick and easy, utterly divine, open-faced pastries made with pre-rolled puff pastry; perfect for getting my fix in a fraction of the time.*

White Cheese & Spinach Open-Faced *Börek*
TRADITIONAL RECIPE, CHEATER'S VERSION

MAKES 4
Prep: 25 minutes
Cook: 20–25 minutes

—

1 x 9–11 oz (250–320 g) sheet of ready-rolled puff pastry (gluten-free is fine)
2 tbsp olive oil + a little more for drizzling
1 large onion, peeled and finely diced
7 oz (200 g) spinach leaves
2 large eggs
1 oz (25 g) fresh flat leaf parsley leaves, finely chopped
2 tsp dried mint
1 tsp *pul biber* (Aleppo pepper/ Turkish red pepper flakes)
A pinch of sea salt flakes and coarse black pepper
7 oz (200 g) *beyaz peynir* (Turkish white cheese)/ feta cheese
1 tsp sesame seeds
¼ tsp nigella seeds
A drizzle of runny honey

Preheat the oven to 425°F (220°C).

Take the puff pastry out of the fridge or freezer to come to room temperature, as per the package instructions.

Add the olive oil to a large frying pan and place on the stove over medium heat. Once hot, add the onion and soften for 10–12 minutes until caramelized. Transfer the onion from the pan to a plate. Add the spinach leaves to the same pan, wilt down completely, then drain in a sieve, squeezing out any excess liquid with the back of a large spoon. Allow the spinach leaves to cool, then roughly chop them.

Whisk together the eggs and add most of them to a large bowl, retaining a tablespoon or so to brush the pastry with later. Add the onion, spinach, parsley, dried mint and *pul biber* to the large bowl, and season with a good pinch of salt and coarse black pepper. Crumble in the *beyaz peynir* with your hands. Using a fork or spoon, mix together well, and leave to one side.

Unroll the puff pastry (which is usually rolled with a piece of oven-safe parchment paper within the packaging, but if yours isn't, roll it out onto a piece of parchment paper, large enough to line a large, shallow baking pan with).

Cut down the middle of the pastry, horizontally and vertically, to create four equal rectangular pieces, then lift the parchment paper with the pastry pieces on it, straight onto your baking pan. Score along the perimeter of each rectangle of pastry, ¾ in (2 cm) in from the edge, and using a fork, prick the center a few times.

Use the reserved egg to brush along the exposed pastry perimeters, sprinkling the seeds along the egg-washed edges. Carefully fill the center of each piece of pastry with equal quantities of the filling, drizzle each *börek* with a little olive oil, then bake in the oven for 20–25 minutes until beautifully golden brown. Drizzle with honey to serve.

I always keep eggs in the fridge for recipes like this; a quick fridge-raid for some sad or leftover veggies and cheese, and I know I'm on my way to quickly making something really delicious. This recipe works equally well with asparagus and/or green beans too. Serve alongside a simple green salad and garlic yogurt (page 109).

Hellim & Sautéed Vegetable Frittata

ALL IN ONE

SERVES 4–6
Prep: 5–10 minutes (using cooked potatoes) or 25 minutes (using uncooked potatoes)
Cook: 15 minutes
—
9 oz (250 g) uncooked baby potatoes or cooked leftover potatoes
5½ oz (150 g) *hellim* (halloumi cheese)
8 large eggs
1 tsp dried mint
1 tsp dried oregano
1 tsp *pul biber* (Aleppo pepper/Turkish red pepper flakes) + extra to finish
1 tsp sea salt flakes
¾ tsp coarse black pepper
1 oz (25 g) fresh cilantro leaves and stalks, finely chopped
3 tbsp olive oil
1 large zucchini, halved lengthways and thinly sliced
9 oz (250 g) chestnut/cremini mushrooms, thinly sliced
2 large scallions, thinly sliced
1 lemon, cut into wedges

If using raw potatoes, wash them, leave them whole and add them to a large pot of cold water. Bring to a boil and cook for 15 minutes, then drain them through a colander. Prepare the rest of the ingredients while the potatoes cook. (If using cooked, leftover potatoes, just skip to the next bit.) Once the boiled and drained potatoes have cooled a little, thickly slice them.

Preheat your broiler to medium-high.

Wash and pat dry the *hellim*, then chop 3½ oz (100 g) of it into small ¾ in (2 cm) cubes, and finely grate the remaining 1¾ oz (50 g).

Whisk together the eggs in a bowl until light and frothy, then add the dried mint, oregano, *pul biber* and half of the sea salt flakes and coarse black pepper. Mix in the fresh cilantro, and leave to one side.

Add most of the olive oil to a large, broiler-safe frying pan and place on the stovetop over medium heat. Once hot, add the cooked, sliced potatoes to the pan and let them crisp up on the underside for a couple of minutes. Add the cubed *hellim*, followed by the zucchini, mushrooms and scallions, but don't stir. Leave the cheese and vegetables to crisp up on their undersides, drizzle with the remaining olive oil, season with the remaining salt and black pepper, stir gently, then leave everything again, without stirring, for another couple of minutes for more crispiness and flavor.

Turn the heat right down, and give the herby eggs another good whisk. Gently stir everything in the pan, then pour in the egg mixture, using a spatula to work quickly to ease the gooey eggs from the perimeter of the pan and into the center. After a couple of minutes, once the edge of the frittata looks like it is starting to set but the center is still quite loose, sprinkle over the grated *hellim* and place the pan under the broiler for 3–5 minutes. Once the top of the frittata starts bubbling and browning, it is ready.

Garnish with *pul biber* and a generous squeeze of fresh lemon juice.

This is one of those quick recipes that I have in my repertoire for when I want to whip up something delicious and full of goodness for breakfast, lunch or dinner. The mushrooms and zucchinis don't take long to crisp up, just don't be tempted to stir them too often, otherwise they'll soften rather than caramelize gloriously.

Crispy Veggie & Mashed Avocado White Cheese on Toast

FAST AND FILLING

SERVES 4
Prep: 10 minutes
Cook: 15 minutes
—

2 medium zucchinis
10½ oz (300 g) chestnut/ cremini mushrooms
7 oz (200 g) *beyaz peynir* **(Turkish white cheese) or feta cheese**
2 large, ripe avocados
1 large unwaxed lemon
   + extra slices to serve
10 large fresh spearmint leaves, finely chopped
½ tsp coarse black pepper
   + extra to garnish
¾ tsp sea salt flakes
3 tbsp extra virgin olive oil
   + extra for drizzling
4 large, thick slices of sourdough bread
2 large garlic cloves, finely grated/crushed
1 tsp dried mint
1 tsp *pul biber* **(Aleppo pepper/ Turkish red pepper flakes)**
   + extra to garnish
4 tbsp mixed seeds (sunflower/pumpkin/sesame)

NOTE
Find my tips for making this in advance on page 24.

Halve the zucchinis lengthways, then slice across, as thinly as possible to create an abundance of semi-circles. Thinly slice the mushrooms, including the stalks.

Using a fork, mash up the white cheese in a large, shallow bowl.

Halve the avocados, remove the stone, slice across the flesh in a criss-cross pattern, then, using a large spoon, scoop out the flesh into the bowl of mashed white cheese. Zest the lemon into the bowl, then cut the lemon in half. Add the juice of one of the lemon halves to the bowl and keep the remaining half for later. Mash everything in the bowl together.

Add the chopped mint and half the black pepper to the bowl, stir, then taste and season with a pinch of the sea salt if necessary.

Add the extra virgin olive oil to the pan and place the pan on the stovetop over medium heat. Once hot, add the zucchinis and mushrooms to the pan, spread them out as evenly as possible, and leave them, without stirring, to crisp up on their undersides.

While the vegetables cook, toast the bread in the toaster, then drizzle with a little more extra virgin olive oil while still hot.

Once the zucchinis and mushrooms have crisped up, give them a stir, flipping as many of them over as possible, and cook for another couple of minutes or so until the other side browns too. Season with the remaining salt and black pepper, stir through the grated or crushed garlic, followed by the dried mint and *pul biber*, cook for another minute or so, squeeze in the juice from the remaining lemon half, then remove the pan from the heat.

Cover each slice of toast with a generous but equal portion of the mashed white cheese and avocado, then a tablespoon each of mixed seeds, then top with the zucchinis and mushrooms. Garnish with a sprinkling of coarse black pepper and *pul biber*, a drizzle of extra virgin olive oil and serve with lemon slices.

A slice of gabira *(grilled village bread or sourdough) simply brushed with olive oil and served with slices of* hellim *(halloumi cheese), black olives, tomatoes, fresh herbs and a hot cup of spiced Cypriot tea is my idea of heaven. So I thought, "Well, how about combining all those delicious flavors into one?" and here you have it! I serve this for a simple lunch snack with friends—just double the quantities, slice the toasts in half or quarters once cooked, and drizzle with honey to create smaller canapé-sized portions.*

Grilled Cypriot Breakfast *Gabira*
FAST AND FILLING

SERVES 4
Prep: 15 minutes
Cook: 10 minutes
—
**4 thick slices of
    sourdough bread**
**3½ oz (100 g) *hellim* (halloumi
    cheese),** coarsely grated
**3½ oz (100 g) *kaşar peyniri*
    or mozzarella cheese,**
    coarsely grated
**2¾ oz (75 g) dry black or
    Kalamata olives,** pitted
    and roughly chopped
1 tsp dried mint
1 oz (25 g) fresh cilantro leaves,
    finely chopped
2 tbsp extra virgin olive oil
3½ oz (100 g) cherry tomatoes,
    sliced
**A good pinch of coarse
    black pepper**
½ tsp toasted sesame seeds
¼ tsp nigella seeds
A drizzle of runny honey
    (optional)

Preheat your broiler to medium-high. Line a large baking pan with parchment paper.

Toast the bread slices in the toaster until lightly golden and place them on the lined baking pan.

While the bread is toasting, mix together the *hellim, kaşar peyniri/* mozzarella cheese, black olives, dried mint and cilantro leaves along with 1 tablespoon of the extra virgin olive oil.

Brush the toasted slices of sourdough with 1 teaspoon of the extra virgin olive oil, then top each one with generous, equal portions of the cheesy olive mixture, as close to the crusts of the bread as possible, reserving a couple of tablespoons for later. Top with the sliced cherry tomatoes, followed by a little more of the reserved cheesy olive mixture and any stray strands of grated cheese and/ or olives that may have fallen onto the baking pan. Finish with a sprinkling of coarse black pepper, sesame and nigella seeds, and a good drizzle of the remaining 2 teaspoons of the extra virgin olive oil.

Place the pan under the broiler for 4–5 minutes until the *kaşar peyniri/*mozzarella cheese melts and the edges of the grated *hellim*, olives and tomatoes caramelize a little. Serve immediately, drizzled with honey (if using), and a hot cup of tea.

Can I let you into a secret? I'm not a huge fan of çılbır, *what the Western world refers to as "Turkish eggs." Sorry, but the poached egg and yogurt combo doesn't do it for me. However, give me a perfectly boiled egg on top of creamy, tangy tahini, drizzled with a spiced* pul biber *butter, contrasted by the crunch of toasted sesame seeds and a fresh, chunky salad, and I'm all yours. In fact, give me a slice of toasted bread to dip into it, and I'm a friend for life. Try this one and I promise you'll be like, "çılbır, who?!"*

Whipped Tahini, Spiced Butter & Boiled Egg Salad

FAST AND FRESH

SERVES 4
Prep: 15 minutes
Cook: 15 minutes
——

1 tbsp sesame seeds
½ cup (150 g) tahini
⅓ cup (75 ml) ice-cold water
⅓ cup (75 ml) freshly squeezed
   lemon juice
4 large garlic cloves,
   crushed or finely grated
1 tsp sea salt flakes
4 large eggs
3½ tbsp unsalted butter
2 tsp *pul biber* (Aleppo pepper/
   Turkish red pepper flakes)
1 tsp smoked paprika
1 small Lebanese, Persian or
   pickling cucumber, or
   ¼ English cucumber
   (deseeded), roughly chopped
1 large, ripe tomato, halved
   and roughly chopped
¼ tsp coarse black pepper
1 tsp dried oregano
¼ oz (10 g) fresh flat leaf parsley
   leaves, very finely chopped

Place a small frying pan on the stovetop over low heat, and toast the sesame seeds, stirring continuously until evenly golden brown all over. Take the pan off the heat and immediately transfer the seeds to a plate so they don't continue cooking.

In a shallow bowl, combine the tahini, ice-cold water, lemon juice and half of the garlic and whisk to a smooth consistency—the mixture will look like it's curdled at first, but don't panic, just keep on whisking until smooth. Add half of the sea salt flakes, whisk again, then leave to one side.

Place the eggs in a small pot, cover with cold water and place on the stovetop over medium heat. Bring up to a boil, simmer for 5 minutes, then take the pot off the heat, carefully drain the hot water and immediately fill up the pot with cold water.

While the eggs are cooking, place the butter, *pul biber*, smoked paprika and remaining garlic into a small pot on the stovetop on low-medium heat, or in a mug in the microwave, and gently stir for a minute or two (or on high for around 30 seconds if using the microwave) until the butter completely melts. Stir well.

Evenly spread the whipped tahini onto four small plates. Once the eggs have been sitting in the pot of cold water for a couple of minutes, peel them, cut them in half and place them with the chopped cucumber and tomato on the whipped tahini. Drizzle the chile butter over the eggs, season the eggs and vegetables generously with the remaining sea salt flakes, the toasted sesame seeds, coarse black pepper, dried oregano and finely chopped parsley, and serve with hot crusty bread or toast.

Mücver are crispy fried fritters, made with grated vegetables such as zucchinis, potatoes or carrots. Years ago, I started making them with sweet potatoes and hellim (halloumi cheese) for every BBQ or gathering we'd host or be invited to. Over time, they've morphed into muffins that are easy to take to picnics and throw into lunchboxes. Sweet potato works perfectly with the salty hellim, and with only a handful of ingredients, they are easy to make, store well in the fridge for up to 3 days (eat cold or heat up) and can be frozen for up to 3 months.

Hellim & Sweet Potato Egg Muffins

TRADITIONAL FLAVORS, NEW RECIPE

MAKES 12
Prep: 10 minutes
Cook: 25–35 minutes

—

14 oz (400 g) sweet potatoes, peeled and finely grated
1 large red onion, peeled and coarsely grated
6 large eggs
3 tbsp extra virgin olive oil
7 oz (200 g) *hellim* (halloumi cheese), coarsely grated
1 oz (30 g) fresh cilantro leaves, finely chopped
2 tsp dried mint
1 tsp *pul biber* (Aleppo pepper/ Turkish red pepper flakes)
¾ tsp coarse black pepper
½ tsp fine sea salt
Scant 1 cup (100 g) self-rising flour

Preheat the oven to 375°F (190°C).

Line a deep 12-hole muffin pan with 12 paper liners.

Squeeze the grated sweet potatoes and onion through a sieve to rid them of any additional liquid. Alternatively, place the grated vegetables into a large cheesecloth and wrap and squeeze tightly until no liquid is being released.

In a large bowl, whisk together the eggs, then mix in all the remaining ingredients, apart from the self-rising flour. Using a sieve, sift in the flour, and fold into the rest of the ingredients, ensuring there are no visible lumps in the batter.

Evenly distribute the mixture into each of the 12 paper liners in the muffin pan—you may find that you need to heap it on, which is fine. Bake on the middle rack of the oven for 25–35 minutes or until the *mücver* muffins are caramelized on top and fully cooked in the center.

Once cooked, carefully remove the muffins from the pan and transfer to a wire rack to cool for a few minutes. Serve warm, or allow to cool and then refrigerate for up to 3 days.

REHEATING INSTRUCTIONS:
If reheating the muffins from frozen, for best results, defrost in the fridge overnight.

Preheated oven: 400°F (200°C), middle shelf, 10–12 minutes, or until piping hot all the way through.
Air fryer: 350°F (180°C), 5–7 minutes, or until piping hot all the way through.
Microwave: High, 30–45 seconds, or until piping hot all the way through.

I've combined my favorite elements of two delicious salads for this one; Kuru Fasulye Salatası/Piyaz and Gavurdağı Salatası. I've also given it the Meliz Cooks touch by adding two of my favorite Cypriot ingredients, hellim (halloumi cheese) and fresh cilantro. This is another great "prepare ahead" salad that stores well in the fridge for up to 3 days, to add to lunches and dinners throughout the week.

Cannellini Bean, Crispy *Hellim* & Crunchy Walnut Salad

FAST AND FRESH

SERVES 4–6
Prep: 15 minutes
Cook: 5 minutes
——

8 oz (225 g) *hellim*
   (halloumi cheese)
3 tbsp extra virgin olive oil
1 x 14 oz (400 g) can cannellini
   beans (8½ oz/240 g drained
   weight), washed and drained
1 oz (25 g) fresh cilantro leaves
   and stalks, finely chopped
Generous 1 cup (200 g)
   pomegranate seeds
2 small Lebanese, Persian or
   pickling cucumbers or
   ⅓ English cucumber
   (deseeded), finely diced
1 large *kapya biber* (capia
   pepper), red romano or
   red bell pepper, halved,
   deseeded and finely diced
2 scallions, thinly sliced
1 tsp sea salt flakes
3 tsp dried mint
2 tsp sumac
2 tsp *pul biber* (Aleppo pepper/
   Turkish red pepper flakes)
3½ oz (100 g) shelled walnuts,
   roughly chopped
2 tbsp pomegranate molasses

Wash the *hellim,* cut it into ½ in (1 cm) cubes and pat the cubes completely dry with paper towels.

Brush a frying pan with 1 tablespoon of the extra virgin olive oil and place the pan on the stovetop over low-medium heat. Once the oil is hot, lightly fry the *hellim* cubes on all sides until golden brown all over. Transfer the fried cubes to a plate lined with paper towels and allow to cool for a few minutes.

Place the cannellini beans, cilantro, pomegranate seeds, cucumber, *kapya biber,* scallions and most of the sea salt flakes, dried mint, sumac, *pul biber* and walnuts (reserving some of the latter five ingredients for garnishing) on a large platter.

Drizzle over the pomegranate molasses and most of the remaining extra virgin olive oil and give everything a good stir. Add the fried *hellim* cubes to the dish, gently toss the salad again, and then garnish with the remaining dried mint, sumac, *pul biber* and walnuts, the rest of the sea salt flakes, and a final generous drizzle of extra virgin olive oil to finish.

This is the kind of salad I eat on repeat. I often make up a big batch, minus the avocado, and keep a jar of the dressing in the fridge so that the salad stays crisp for a few days. I then add the fresh avocado, a different protein and a drizzle of the dressing each day for lunch. It works particularly well with boiled eggs, and/ or canned tuna, smoked fish, such as mackerel, or roasted salmon fillets. Once prepared, if you decide to keep the salad in the fridge, let it cool before refrigerating, then eat the salad fridge-cold for the next 3 days.

Loaded Pasta, Grain or Rice Salad

FAST AND FRESH

SERVES 2–4
Prep: 10 minutes
Cook: 5 minutes
—

4 tbsp extra virgin olive oil
2 tbsp red wine vinegar
2 tbsp freshly squeezed
  lemon juice
1 tsp sea salt flakes
2 tsp dried mint
1 small Lebanese, Persian
  or pickling cucumber,
  or ¼ English cucumber
  (deseeded), roughly chopped
3½ oz (100 g) cherry or baby
  plum tomatoes, finely sliced
2 large scallions, finely sliced
1¾ oz (50 g) fresh cilantro
  leaves and stalks, finely
  chopped
9 oz (250 g) cooked brown rice,
  orzo or quinoa, piping hot
2 tsp nigella seeds
2 tsp sesame seeds
1 tbsp sunflower seeds
1 tbsp pumpkin seeds
1 small ripe avocado, pitted,
  peeled and finely chopped

TIP
See my tips for prepping this one in advance on page 25.

Combine the extra virgin olive oil, red wine vinegar, lemon juice, sea salt flakes and dried mint in a small jar, close the lid tightly and shake the jar vigorously so that the dressing ingredients emulsify and thicken.

Combine the cucumber, tomatoes, scallions, fresh cilantro, piping hot grains and all of the seeds in a large mixing bowl. Shake the dressing vigorously again, and pour it over the salad. Add the avocado, gently stir again and serve immediately. If there are any leftovers, allow to cool and refrigerate.

NOTES
Adding hot rice, grains or pasta to the salad allows the flavors in the dressing to really get into those grains. You can use hot, cooked microwaveable brown rice or quinoa for ease, or cook up a batch of orzo, brown rice or quinoa yourself on the stovetop following the package instructions.

If I make this in advance, I simply prepare the mixed salad and refrigerate, but forego adding the hot grains, avocado and dressing until just before serving.

This is such a quick and easy recipe to get the kids involved with, and my son especially takes pride in independently cooking this meal for us at home. You can use microwaveable brown rice for ease, or leftover cooked rice, and feel free to improvise with whatever vegetables you have in your fridge and freezer; the ones I use here are simply the ones we regularly have in ours.

"Throw It All In" Egg-Fried Rice
FAST AND FILLING

SERVES 4
Prep: 10 minutes
Cook: 10 minutes
—

3 tbsp olive oil
2 tbsp sesame seeds
2 tbsp fresh ginger, peeled and finely grated
1 tbsp garlic cloves, peeled and finely grated or crushed
4 scallions, finely sliced
1 *kapya biber* (capia pepper), red romano or small red bell pepper, halved, deseeded and cut into 1¼ in (3 cm) pieces
9 oz (250 g) chestnut/cremini mushrooms, sliced
1 medium zucchini, halved lengthways, finely sliced into semi-circles
2 cups (150 g) shredded savoy or sweetheart cabbage, finely shredded
1 cup (100 g) frozen edamame beans
3 cups (500 g) cooked brown rice, or 2 x 9 oz (250 g) packages cooked microwave brown rice
4 large eggs
2 tbsp dark soy sauce
1 oz (25 g) fresh cilantro leaves, roughly chopped
1 tsp *pul biber* (Aleppo pepper/ Turkish red pepper flakes)
Kimchi/hot sauce, to serve

Add 2 tablespoons of the olive oil to a large, deep frying pan and place on the stovetop over medium heat. Once the oil is hot, add the sesame seeds, ginger and garlic to the pan and stir for 30 seconds or so until the ingredients start to release their aroma. Add the scallions and cook for another 30 seconds before adding the *kapya biber*, mushrooms, zucchini, cabbage and edamame beans to the pan. Cook over high heat for 4–5 minutes until the edges of the vegetables start to char a little, stirring every now and then.

Add the cooked brown rice to the pan, stir until piping hot, turn the heat down low and push the cooked ingredients to one side of the pan. Drizzle in the remaining tablespoon of olive oil into the empty space in the pan, and once hot, quickly crack in the eggs, and using a wooden spoon, vigorously whisk the egg whites and yolks together. Once the eggs start to stiffen but are still runny, stir them through the vegetable fried rice, drizzle over the soy sauce, take the pan off the heat and serve immediately with the fresh cilantro, a sprinkling of *pul biber*, and either some kimchi or hot sauce (of choice) on the side.

Balık Ekmek, which literally translates as "fish bread" in Turkish, is a popular street food, found typically in the Eminönü area of Istanbul, Türkiye. Fresh mackerel is cooked over hot coals, then placed into fresh sandwich baguettes or Somun Ekmeği with an array of salad vegetables. I usually have a package of smoked mackerel in the fridge and find it easier to make Balık Ekmek at home with these. If you really fancy pushing the boat out (excuse the pun), you can make your own mini Somun Ekmeği by leaving out the sesame seeds from the recipe on page 191 and dividing the dough into four instead of two, as a more authentic alternative to store-bought baguettes.

Balık Ekmek-Style Smoked Mackerel Baguettes

TRADITIONAL RECIPE, CHEATER'S VERSION

SERVES 4
Prep: 10 minutes
Cook: 15 minutes

——

¼ cup (60 g) mayonnaise
1 large unwaxed lemon, zested and cut into 4 wedges
½ tsp dried mint
½ tsp coarse black pepper
4 large smoked mackerel fillets
4 small, fresh sandwich baguettes
1¾ oz (50 g) arugula leaves
1 large white onion, peeled, halved and finely sliced
1 kapya biber (capia pepper), red romano or small red bell pepper, halved, deseeded and finely sliced
1 oz (30 g) fresh flat leaf parsley leaves, finely chopped
2 large, ripe tomatoes, thinly sliced
1 tsp sumac
2 tbsp pomegranate molasses
½ tsp sea salt flakes
4 pickles, thinly sliced
1 tsp pul biber (Aleppo pepper/ Turkish red pepper flakes)

Preheat the oven to 375°F (190°C). Line a large, shallow baking pan with parchment paper.

In a small bowl, mix together the mayonnaise, lemon zest, dried mint and coarse black pepper, and leave to one side.

Place the mackerel fillets on one end of the lined baking pan. Splash the baguettes with a little bit of cold water, and place them on the other end of the pan. Bake on the middle rack of your oven for 10–12 minutes or until the fish is piping hot. If the baguettes look like they are browning too much, remove them from the oven before the fish.

While the fish and bread are in the oven, prepare the salad. Place the arugula, onion, *kapya biber*, parsley, tomatoes and sumac in a large dish but do not stir until the fish and bread are ready.

Take the pan out of the oven and use a knife and fork to carefully peel away the skin of the mackerel. Break the flesh into pieces.

Drizzle the salad with the pomegranate molasses, sprinkle on the sea salt and lightly toss together.

Slice the baguettes in half lengthways, and spread the prepared mayonnaise on the inside of each of the four top halves of the baguettes. Generously load the bottom half of each of the four baguettes with the salad, then top with the sliced pickles and finally the hot, smoked mackerel. Squeeze the juice from the lemon wedges over the mackerel, then sprinkle each sandwich with a little *pul biber*. Place the tops of the baguette on the sandwiches and devour your *balık ekmek*.

A favorite kitsch Christmas Dinner appetizer, this humble seafood cocktail with a twist makes a delicious and very quick meal. The filling takes all of 10 minutes to put together and can be used to fill pita bread, top a baked potato, or stir it through cold pasta to make a pasta salad.

Seafood Cocktail Pita Pockets

FAST AND FRESH

SERVES 4
Prep: 10 minutes
—

2 unwaxed lemons
1 cup (120 g) mayonnaise
2 tsp *tatlı biber salçası*
    (Turkish sweet/mild
    red pepper paste)
2 tsp pomegranate molasses
½ tsp smoked paprika
2 tsp *pul biber* (Aleppo
    pepper/Turkish red pepper
    flakes) + extra to finish
¾ tsp sea salt flakes
½ tsp coarse black pepper
    + extra to finish
10½ oz (300 g) cooked king
    shrimp, whole, shells
    and tails off
8 seafood sticks,
    roughly chopped
6 radishes, finely sliced
1 small Lebanese, Persian
    or pickling cucumber, or
    ¼ English cucumber
    (deseeded), roughly chopped
2 large scallions,
    finely sliced
1 small cos/baby gem lettuce,
    finely shredded
1 ripe avocado, pitted, peeled
    and cut into ¾ in (2 cm) dice
4 large, soft pita breads,
    kept whole but sliced open
    along the top

Zest one of the lemons and cut it in half.

In a large bowl, whisk together the lemon zest, mayonnaise, *tatlı biber salçası*, pomegranate molasses, smoked paprika, *pul biber*, sea salt flakes and coarse black pepper.

Devein the shrimp and cut a light slit along the back of each on

e, which will encourage more of the sauce to get into them. Pat the shrimp dry with paper towels and add them to the sauce along with the seafood sticks, and give everything a gentle stir. Mix through the radishes, cucumber and scallions and ensure the shredded lettuce is completely dry before adding to the mixture too.

Finally, squeeze in the lemon juice from the lemon halves, stir through the avocado, then generously load each pita bread with the seafood cocktail filling. Sprinkle with a little more coarse black pepper and *pul biber*. Cut the remaining lemon into 4 wedges and serve one with each pita.

LEFTOVERS & PANTRY

Having the confidence to know how to effectively utilize leftovers, a few odds and ends from the fridge, and ingredients from a well-stocked pantry, is one of the most useful skills to have in the home kitchen. I love the satisfaction of making something out of nothing and never wasting a scrap. This chapter is about making the most out of the essential pantry ingredients I mention on pages 15 to 21, to ensure you are always on your way to creating a flavorful meal. These recipes can be made with dried and canned ingredients and showcase some of my favorites, such as Tomatoey Caramelized Onions & Beans (page 68), Nutty, Herby Brown Rice & Lentils (page 55) and Charred Greens & Pantry Beans (page 58).

There are hearty and comforting soups and broths, filling lentil, rice and pasta dishes, and of course, my Creamy Dreamy Hummus recipe (page 63). I'm a firm believer that with a can of chickpeas and a jar of tahini, you will never go hungry and will always be satisfied.

So, let's take a minute to talk about hummus. Every family occasion, BBQ, picnic, family dinner and breakfast (yes, breakfast) table I remember as a child was enhanced by the addition of my mom's homemade hummus. My mom would use the leftovers to make Hummus Soup (page 67), especially if my dad's dad, Ali Dede, was coming over. Hummus reminds me of good times, celebrations, weddings, beautifully adorned mezze tables. The truth is, once you make your own batch of proper tahini-laden homemade hummus, going back to store-bought will feel like you're doing yourself and the entire homemade-hummus-making community a disservice. I mean, I would go so far as to say that simply using hummus to dip crudités into is sacrilegious in my family's eyes! Beautifying hummus by loading it with a deliciously dressed salad (page 65) or some humble vegetables that have been roasted with a few simple pantry spices (page 64), elevates this popular dip into a delicious meal in itself.

There is one dish in this chapter that reminds me of school breaks, and it's my mom's şehriyeli çorba (vermicelli soup). This Vermicelli Soup with Fried *Hellim* (page 57) is a recipe that requires zero peeling, prepping or chopping (other than a few cubes of *hellim*), and has become one of my go-to lunches when I'm juggling working while the kids are at home, exactly as my mom would do.

We use durum wheat vermicelli to make this soup, and it's important to slowly toast the pasta in oil first, before boiling it, to prevent the cooked soup from having a "slimy" texture. Toasting the vermicelli also gives the pasta, and the soup, a warmer, and somewhat nuttier flavor. I use the same technique when toasting orzo, as in the Caramelized Onion & Orzo Basmati Rice (page 121).

Traditionally in Turkish-Cypriot cuisine, fried *hellim* (halloumi) is served with *tarhana çorbası* (a creamy soup made from rusks of combined dried, kibbled wheat and fermented milk or yogurt) but my mom would always add this to şehriyeli çorba and any other thick and soupy pasta dishes she'd make for us. Try it on any of the pasta and soup dishes in this chapter, for example, the *Ezogelin* Soup (page 52), Creamy *Hellim* & Tomato Orzo (page 60) and the Chicken, Leek & Pasta Broth (page 70).

Cooking with Brown Rice Vermicelli

To make Vermicelli Soup *(page 57) and* Caramelized Onion & Orzo Basmati Rice *(page 121) gluten free.*

I favor brown rice vermicelli over the white rice version, purely for its lovely depth of color once toasted, and its nuttier flavor, which makes it more similar to that of durum wheat vermicelli.

◉ Dry brown rice vermicelli usually comes in slabs, and so you'll need to gently crush the slabs to create small, individual strands of vermicelli, each around 1¼ in (3 cm) long.

◉ When frying the small strands of rice vermicelli in oil, ensure to do this over the lowest heat possible so that the strands brown slowly rather than puffing up. Do not be tempted to turn up the heat or rush the process, as not only will the vermicelli strands puff and expand, resulting in a mushy texture once boiled, but having the heat up too high will force you to continuously stir the rice vermicelli to prevent them from burning, which will only break them up further into tiny little shards.

◉ The toasted brown rice vermicelli strands should be a rich, golden-brown color. Once toasted, you can follow the process of making the Vermicelli Soup exactly following the main recipe.

◉ If you are using the brown rice vermicelli as a substitute for the orzo in the Caramelized Onion & Orzo Basmati Rice, then follow the same toasting instructions given for the brown rice vermicelli. Transfer all of the toasted vermicelli from the pot to a plate. Add the butter to the pot and soften the onion in the butter until golden and caramelized. Allow the onion to cool down, return the toasted rice vermicelli to the pot and follow the rest of the method exactly as stated in the main recipe.

Legend has it that Ezo Gelin *(translating as "Ezo the bride") made this soup to impress her in-laws; and let me tell you, this soup is one to impress, both in its brevity and unassuming simplicity. This is a recipe I always have plenty of lemons in the fridge for, and a loaf of* Susamlı Somun Ekmeği *(page 191) in the freezer, ready to heat up and dip into it. It tastes better the next day and the day after, and freezes well too. I like adding a pinch of smoked paprika to my unconventional recipe for a little sweetness and warmth. You can make this with the traditional bulgur, or if you'd prefer to keep it gluten free, simply swap the bulgur for quinoa.*

Ezogelin Soup

ALL IN ONE

SERVES 6–8
Prep: 10 minutes
Cook: 45–50 minutes

—

1½ cups (300 g) **dried red lentils**
3 tbsp **white rice** (short-grain/
    pudding rice is best but any
    white rice will do)
scant ½ cup (60 g) dry, coarse
    bulgur or dried quinoa
1 **vegetable stock cube,**
    crumbled
2 cups (500 ml) **boiling
    hot water** + 10½ cups
    (2.5 liters) **cold water**
3 tbsp **olive oil**
1 **large onion,** peeled and
    finely diced
1 **large carrot,** peeled and
    finely diced
1 **large celery stick,** finely diced
1 tsp **sea salt flakes**
    + extra to serve
1 tsp **paprika**
½ tsp **smoked paprika**
1 tsp *pul biber* **(Aleppo pepper/
    Turkish red pepper flakes)**
    + extra to serve
2 tbsp *tatlı biber salçası*
    **(Turkish sweet/mild
    red pepper paste)**
1 tbsp **tomato paste**
1 tbsp **dried mint** + extra to serve
1 tsp **coarse black pepper**
    + extra to serve
Juice of 1 large lemon

Wash and drain the lentils, rice and bulgur/quinoa in a sieve until the water runs clear (around a minute) and leave to drain over a bowl.

In a large jug, whisk together the stock cube and boiling water, and once dissolved, top up with 2 cups (500 ml) of the cold water.

Add the olive oil to a large soup pot or Dutch oven and place on the stovetop over low-medium heat. Once hot, add the onion, carrot and celery to the pot, along with the sea salt, and cook the vegetables for 10–12 minutes until soft and jammy. Sprinkle in the paprika, smoked paprika and *pul biber*, stir well, then add the *tatlı biber salçası* and tomato paste to the pot, and cook them down for a couple of minutes, stirring continuously.

Next, add the drained lentils, rice and bulgur/quinoa to the pot and stir well into the rest of the ingredients. Pour in the 4¼ cups (1 liter) of prepared stock and the additional 8½ cups (2 liters) of cold water to the pot, and give everything a good stir. Turn up the heat, bring the soup up to a rolling boil, then simmer on low heat for around 25–30 minutes until it has thickened and reduced, ensuring to skim off and discard the foam that naturally forms on top of the bubbling liquid. Once you have discarded the foam, stir in the dried mint and coarse black pepper.

Turn off the heat, add most of the lemon juice to the pot, stir and taste. Serve with an extra sprinkling of dried mint, black pepper, *pul biber* and more fresh lemon juice, seasoning with more salt to taste.

Now, there are two ways you can make this rice—you can cook the brown rice and lentils together in stock using the absorption method, or you can use a can of green lentils and two packages of microwaveable rice, leaving out the cooking in stock completely. I've given you both options, but just bear in mind that cooking the dried rice and lentils in stock is the more flavorful method. This is delicious served with the Juicy Köfte & Spinach Stew *(page 92) or the* Pomegranate-Orange Chicken & Potatoes *(page 84).*

Nutty, Herby Brown Rice & Lentils
ALL IN ONE

SERVES 4–6 (GENEROUSLY)
Prep: 10 minutes (dry method)
Cook: 50 minutes (dry method);
10 minutes (cooked method)
———

1 **vegetable stock cube** (if using the dry method), crumbled
8¾ **cups (900 ml) boiling hot water** (only needed for the dry method)
¾ **cup (150 g) dried green lentils or 2 x 14 oz (400 g) cans brown lentils (8½ oz/240 g drained weight)**, drained and rinsed
1⅓ **cups (150 g) uncooked long-grain brown rice, or 2 x 9 oz (250 g) packages cooked microwave brown rice**
⅓ **cup (50 g) pine nuts**
⅓ **cup (50 g) blanched almonds**
2 **tbsp sesame seeds**
3 **tbsp olive oil**
4 **large scallions,** finely sliced
4 **large garlic cloves,** crushed or finely grated (around 1 heaped tsp)
1 **tsp ground cumin**
1 **tsp sea salt flakes**
1 **tsp coarse black pepper**
2 **tsp dried mint**
2 **tsp** *pul biber* **(Aleppo pepper/ Turkish red pepper flakes)**
1 **oz (25 g) fresh cilantro leaves and stalks,** finely chopped
Lemon wedges, to serve

Dry Rice & Lentil Method: Place the crumbled stock cube and the boiling hot water in a jug and stir until fully dissolved. Leave to one side. Lay the dried lentils out on a large tray and check for any stones or duds and discard. Add the rice and lentils to a large sieve and wash under cold running water until the water runs clear. Set the sieve to drain over a bowl.

Add the pine nuts, blanched almonds and sesame seeds to a large sauté pan and place over medium heat. Stirring continuously, toast until golden brown, then immediately transfer the nuts and seeds to a plate. Wipe the pan with paper towels.

Place the pan back on the stovetop over medium heat, pour in the olive oil, and once hot, add half of the sliced scallions to the pan and soften for a couple of minutes. Add the garlic and ground cumin, stir for a minute or two, then add the drained rice and lentils, stirring to coat them in the onion and garlic-infused oil. Pour in the stock, sprinkle in half of the sea salt flakes and bring up to a boil, then turn the heat right down, put the lid on and cook for around 30 minutes.

The liquid should be fully absorbed once the lentils are cooked. Take the pan off the heat, remove the lid and place a large sheet of paper towel over the pan. Pop the lid back on and leave for 10 minutes.

Place the rice and lentils into a large, shallow dish, add in the remaining ingredients, stir well and serve with lemon wedges.

Cooked Rice & Lentil Method: *Toast the nuts and seeds as above and remove. Using the same pot, soften the scallions in the olive oil, as above, then add the garlic and cumin and soften for another minute or so until fragrant. Add the pre-cooked (microwave) brown rice and drained lentils to the pot and heat through, stirring continuously until the rice and lentils are piping hot. Place everything from the pot into a large, shallow dish, and add in the remaining ingredients, stir well and serve with lemon wedges.*

It's such a treat to slurp up a mouthful of these toasted golden brown noodles and the minty, lemony broth while biting into a crunchy, yet squidgy piece of crispy, golden hellim *(halloumi cheese) at the same time. This simple soup can be made gluten free (see page 51) and is delicious served with grilled black olives; although nothing else is really needed, if you did want to dip some bread into the juicies, it's preferable to toast it first.*

Vermicelli Soup with Fried *Hellim*
FAST AND FILLING

SERVES 4
Prep: 5 minutes
Cook: 25 minutes
—

1 chicken or vegetable stock cube, crumbled
1 tbsp tomato paste
1 tbsp *tatlı biber salçası* (Turkish sweet/mild red pepper paste)
8¾ cups (900 ml) boiling hot water
4 tbsp olive oil
5½ oz (150 g) dried durum wheat vermicelli, broken into 1¼ in (3 cm) strands
1 tsp dried mint + extra to garnish
1 tsp *pul biber* (Aleppo pepper/ Turkish red pepper flakes) + extra to garnish
½ tsp sea salt flakes
½ tsp coarse black pepper + extra to garnish
5½ oz (150 g) *hellim* (halloumi cheese), washed and cut into ¾ in (2 cm) cubes
1 large lemon, juiced + extra to serve

NOTE
See page 50 for why I fry the vermicelli.

In a large jug, whisk the crumbled stock cube, the tomato purée and *tatlı biber salçası* into the boiling water until dissolved. Leave to one side.

Add 3 tablespoon of the olive oil to a large pot and place on the stovetop over low heat. Once hot, add the vermicelli to the pan and fry for a couple of minutes, stirring continuously so that each strand browns evenly. Once the vermicelli strands are a rich golden-brown color, take the pot off the heat. The vermicelli will continue to darken a little once removed from the heat.

Allow the vermicelli to cool down in the pot for a few minutes (to prevent the oil and liquid from reacting and dangerously splattering when the stock is added), then carefully pour in the stock mixture.

Place the pot back on the stovetop over medium heat, stir through the dried mint, *pul biber*, sea salt flakes and coarse black pepper, bring the soup up to a boil, then simmer on low-medium heat for 10–12 minutes until the vermicelli is cooked but still has a little bit of a bite to it (add another ½–¾ cup/120–180 ml of boiling water to the pot while it's cooking if you feel like the soup needs loosening a little).

Brush a small frying pan with the remaining 1 tablespoon of olive oil and place the pan on the stovetop over medium heat. Pat the *hellim* cubes dry with paper towels and carefully add the cubes to the hot oil. Cook the cubes for a couple of minutes, ensuring to turn them frequently until the cubes are a lovely golden-brown color all over. Remove to a plate lined with paper towels (to soak up excess oil).

Once the soup is ready, stir through the lemon juice, take the pot off the heat and let it rest for 5 minutes. Ladle into bowls, add the crispy *hellim* cubes, sprinkle over a little more dried mint, *pul biber* and coarse black pepper, and a squeeze of lemon juice to taste.

I was never that kid that didn't eat their vegetables. I love the stuff. However, sautéing some simple greens in olive oil, softening them in stock and then flavoring them with simple pantry herbs and spices means that I now REALLY LOVE the stuff. This dish can be made in advance and reheated on the stovetop or in the oven (with a little extra liquid) the next day, or even eaten cold.

Charred Greens & Pantry Beans

FAST AND FILLING

SERVES 4–6
Prep: 5 minutes
Cook: 15 minutes
—

1 chicken or vegetable stock cube, crumbled
1⅔ cups (400 ml) boiling hot water
1 x sweetheart cabbage (approx. 1 lb 2 oz–1 lb 5 oz/ 500–600 g)
2 tbsp olive oil
2 large garlic cloves, finely grated
½ tsp coriander seeds, lightly crushed + a little more to garnish
1 tsp dried mint + a little more to garnish
1 tsp *pul biber* (Aleppo pepper/ Turkish red pepper flakes) + a little more to garnish
¼ tsp coarse black pepper, + a little more to garnish
1 x 14 oz (400 g) can butter beans (8½ oz/240 g drained weight), drained and rinsed
A pinch of sea salt flakes
Extra virgin olive oil, to drizzle

NOTE
The sauce is crying out to be dipped into with the Simple Seeded Loaves (page 191), so have a couple of hot crusty loaves in the oven ready for this one. It is also delicious served with the Creamy Haydari (page 126) or Mütebbel (page 128).

In a jug, whisk the crumbled stock cube into the boiling water until fully dissolved, and leave to one side.

Halve the cabbage lengthways, then halve each half lengthways again so you end up with four equal-sized wedges. Wash and pat dry. Add 1 tablespoon of the olive oil to a large sauté pan and place on the largest burner over the highest heat. Once hot, add the cabbage wedges to the pot, placing them into the hot oil with one of the flat sides facing downwards. Cook for a couple of minutes or until the undersides char, then flip them over onto their other cut sides for another couple of minutes until charred.

Move the cabbage wedges to one side of the pan and pour in the remaining 1 tablespoon of olive oil to the vacant side. Add the garlic and crushed coriander seeds to the hot oil, stir immediately to ensure the garlic doesn't burn, then pour in half (a scant 1 cup/200 ml) of the stock. Sprinkle in the dried mint, *pul biber* and black pepper, stir, then move the wedges into the stock, cut sides facing downwards. Cook on the highest heat until the stock reduces and thickens.

After a couple of minutes, move the cabbage wedges to one side again, add the drained butter beans to the pan, giving them a gentle stir in the sticky stock. Pour in the remaining stock, and when the liquid starts to vigorously bubble again, move the wedges back to the center of the pan on their other cut side, spooning over the juices from the pan while the stock reduces.

After a couple of minutes, and once you are left with a thickened, but pourable, sauce, serve everything onto a large platter, spooning the sticky stock over the cabbage and beans. The cabbage should be soft, charred and sticky, and the beans fully coated in the deliciously thick, herby sauce.

Garnish with *pul biber*, dried mint and crushed coriander seeds, season with the sea salt flakes and more coarse black pepper, and serve with a generous drizzle of extra virgin olive oil.

My family and I LOVE this dish, and it was a favorite of mine growing up too. The flavor combination of sweet sautéed vegetables, tomatoes, grated hellim (halloumi cheese) and dried mint is just heavenly, and the final texture should be loose and creamy, and on your dinner table in about 30 minutes. To really save on time, I store bags of finely chopped onions, carrots and celery in the freezer (see tips on page 8) so that I can just throw them straight into the pan without any additional prep.

Creamy *Hellim* & Tomato Orzo

ALL IN ONE

SERVES 4–6
Prep: 5 minutes
Cook: 30 minutes
—

4½ oz (125 g) *hellim*
  (halloumi cheese),
  finely grated
1 tbsp dried mint
½ tsp coarse black pepper
1 vegetable stock cube,
  crumbled
2 cups (500 ml) boiling
  hot water
3 tbsp olive oil
1 large onion, peeled and
  finely diced
2 carrots, peeled and finely diced
2 celery sticks, finely diced
½ tsp sea salt flakes
3 garlic cloves, finely
  grated/crushed
¼ tsp ground cinnamon
1 tsp *pul biber* (Aleppo pepper/
  Turkish red pepper flakes)
  + extra to finish
1 tbsp tomato paste
1 tbsp *tatlı biber salçası*
  (Turkish sweet/mild
  red pepper paste)
1½ cups (300 g) dried orzo
1 x 14 oz (400 g) can
  chopped tomatoes

Mix the grated *hellim* with the dried mint and ¼ teaspoon of the black pepper, and leave to one side.

In a large jug, whisk the crumbled stock cube into the boiling water until dissolved, and leave to one side.

Add the olive oil to a large, nonstick sauté pan and place over medium heat. Once hot, add the finely diced onion, carrots and celery to the pan, sprinkle in the sea salt flakes and soften for at least 8–10 minutes or until the vegetables start turning translucent and begin to caramelize around the edges. Add the garlic, stir for a minute or so until it starts to release its aroma, then stir through the ground cinnamon and *pul biber*.

Stir the tomato paste and *tatlı biber salçası* into the jammy vegetables, followed by the orzo and remaining black pepper, gently stirring so that all the tomatoey deliciousness in the pan coats the pasta. Pour in the can of chopped tomatoes, stir well and turn down the heat. Top up the empty can of chopped tomatoes with cold water, add it to the jug of 2 cups (500 ml) of stock from earlier so that the volume of the liquid in the jug reaches 4¼ cups (1 liter) in total.

Pour the 4¼ cups (1 liter) of stock into the pan, stir well and cook on very low heat for 12–15 minutes, stirring every now and then so that the orzo doesn't stick to the bottom of the pan, but not too often as the strands of orzo could end up breaking.

Once the pasta is ready, stir through half of the grated *hellim* and dried mint mixture, then spoon into bowls and top with the remaining *hellim* mixture and a sprinkling of *pul biber*.

The popularity of my loaded hummus recipes has, in all honesty, blown my mind. Here, I've shared my hummus recipe, which I recommend making with deliciously plump jarred chickpeas or boiling up your own for a much creamier hummus, along with two loaded topping ideas and my mom's very tasty hummus soup recipe.

Creamy Dreamy Hummus

FAST AND FRESH

MAKES 8–10 SERVINGS
Prep: 5 minutes

—

1 x 1 lb 7½ oz (660 g) jar chickpeas or 3 cups (500 g) cooked chickpeas
1 tsp finely chopped garlic cloves
Scant ½ cup (100 g) tahini
1 tbsp extra virgin olive oil
½ tsp sea salt flakes (or more to taste)
⅓ cup (80 ml) freshly squeezed lemon juice (or more to taste)
A little ice-cold water to loosen the mixture if necessary

Place the chickpeas into a blender. If the aquafaba (the chickpea liquid) in the jar is thick and gloopy, throw the entire contents of the jar into the blender—if it is watery, drain the liquid from the jar, but reserve it for later.

Add the remaining ingredients, other than the ice-cold water, to the blender. Blend, and if the mixture is too thick, loosen it by adding a tablespoon of either the reserved liquid (aquafaba) or a spoonful of ice-cold water at a time, until the hummus reaches a smooth and creamy consistency to your liking. Taste and add a little more salt or lemon juice if required. The hummus will keep, covered, in the fridge for up to 3 days.

NOTE

If you would like to cook your own chickpeas, then use 1¾ cups (300 g) dried chickpeas to make approximately 3⅔ cups (600 g) cooked chickpeas. Follow the package instructions but do ensure to add 1 tbsp baking soda to the water while the chickpeas cook (to help soften the skins). I wait for the chickpeas to cool before using them to make hummus. Feel free to remove the skins from the cooled, cooked chickpeas for an even creamier hummus.

I roast the cauliflower, potatoes and chickpeas in the oven for this recipe, but you can use an air fryer (see page 201); just ensure to roast in two batches if using the latter, to ensure full crispiness. Delicious served with the Crispy Chicken Wings (see page 106) and Ocakbaşı-Style Salad (see page 122). Photo of each loaded hummus on page 62.

Loaded Hummus Topping No. 1: Spiced Roasted Cauliflower, Potatoes & Chickpeas

ALL IN ONE

SERVES 4-6
Prep: 15 minutes
Cook: 30–35 minutes
——

4 tbsp olive oil
1 x 14 oz (400 g) can chickpeas (8½ oz/240 g drained weight)
14 oz (400 g) baby potatoes, washed and halved
14 oz (400 g) cauliflower florets
2 tbsp cornstarch
1 tsp sumac + extra to garnish
1 tsp ground cumin + extra to garnish
2 tsp paprika + extra to garnish
1 tsp *pul biber* (Aleppo pepper/Turkish red pepper flakes) + extra to garnish
2 tsp garlic powder
1 tsp sea salt flakes
½ tsp coarse black pepper
2 tsp dried oregano
1 tbsp sesame seeds
1 batch of Creamy Dreamy Hummus (page 63)
A small handful of fresh parsley leaves, finely chopped
1 tbsp extra virgin olive oil

Preheat the oven to 425°F (220°C).

Brush a large, nonstick baking pan with 1 tablespoon of olive oil and put it in the oven for 10 minutes while you prepare the ingredients.

Wash and drain the chickpeas through a sieve, place them on a large baking pan lined with a couple of sheets of paper towels, and pat and roll them as dry as possible with another couple of sheets of paper towels. Pat the potatoes and cauliflower florets dry with paper towels too—this will prevent the chickpeas and vegetables from releasing too much moisture while cooking, allowing them to crisp up beautifully.

Add the chickpeas, potatoes and cauliflower to a large bowl, sprinkle over the cornstarch and mix well with clean hands until fully coated—shaking the bowl a few times helps too.

Add 2 tablespoons of the olive oil to the bowl along with the sumac, cumin, paprika, *pul biber* and garlic powder and mix again. Add the remaining olive oil, the sea salt flakes, coarse black pepper, oregano and sesame seeds, and stir well again, shaking the bowl, to ensure everything is fully coated.

Add the contents of the bowl evenly to the hot pan (the oil should sizzle), placing the potatoes cut-side down, then put the pan back in the oven (in between the middle and top racks).

Roast for 30–35 minutes, turning the potatoes and cauliflower over halfway through (if some of the cauliflower florets start browning too much, remove them from the pan sooner), until everything is cooked through and crispy all over.

While the vegetables and chickpeas are in the oven, make the hummus, then spread it all over a large platter. Top with the roasted vegetables and a sprinkling of sumac, cumin, paprika, *pul biber* and fresh parsley, and a generous drizzle of extra virgin olive oil.

Loaded Hummus Topping No. 2: Finely Chopped Salad

FAST AND FRESH

SERVES 4–6
Prep: 10 minutes
___

⅓ cup (50 g) pine nuts
2 small Lebanese, Persian or pickling cucumber, or ⅓ English cucumber, deseeded
1 *kapya biber* (capia pepper), red romano or small red bell pepper, halved and deseeded
2 scallions
1 oz (25 g) fresh cilantro leaves
½ cup (100 g) pomegranate seeds
½ tsp dried mint
1 tbsp extra virgin olive oil
2 tsp pomegranate molasses
¼ tsp sea salt flakes
1 batch of Creamy Dreamy Hummus (page 63), reserve 1 heaped tbsp of chickpeas before making the hummus

To garnish:
Paprika
Sumac
Pul biber (Aleppo pepper/ Turkish red pepper flakes)
Ground cumin
Extra virgin olive oil

Place the pine nuts in a small frying pan over low-medium heat, and toast them for a few minutes, gently moving the pan around so that they color as evenly as possible. Take the pan off the heat and transfer the pine nuts to a cold dish so they don't continue to darken in color in the hot pan.

Finely dice and chop the cucumber, *kapya biber*, scallions and cilantro leaves, and mix together with the pomegranate seeds, reserving a few cilantro leaves and pomegranate seeds to garnish the hummus with.

Dress the salad with the dried mint, extra virgin olive oil and pomegranate molasses, and season with sea salt flakes just before serving.

Spread the hummus onto a large plate or platter and garnish with the reserved chickpeas, a pinch each of paprika, sumac, *pul biber* and cumin, a generous drizzle of extra virgin olive oil, and top with the salad, the reserved cilantro leaves and pomegranate seeds and the toasted pine nuts.

This soup was my paternal grandfather, Ali Dede's, favorite soup and my dad's family were renowned for cooking and serving it in their village café in Terazi *(Zygi),* Kıbrıs *(Cyprus). It's traditionally made with freshly boiled chickpeas, but I'm sharing with you my cheater's version, and more of a tip, for using up leftover hummus. It's also a great way of clearing out the blender when making hummus; add freshly boiled (but not boiling hot) water to the blender to release any hummus stuck to the bottom, then pour this into your pot for zero wastage. I do not advise making this with store-bought hummus at all—homemade is the only way.*

Hummus Soup
TRADITIONAL RECIPE, CHEATER'S VERSION

SERVES 4
Prep: 5 minutes
Cook: 5–10 minutes
——
2 slices of thick stale bread
2½ cups (600 g) Creamy Dreamy
   Hummus (see page 63)
1½ cups (350 ml) boiling hot
   water
2 tbsp olive oil

To garnish:
Sumac
Pul biber (Aleppo pepper/
   Turkish red pepper flakes)
Paprika
Ground cumin
Fresh flat leaf parsley leaves,
   finely chopped
Dry black olives
Extra virgin olive oil

Cut the stale bread into 1¼ in (3 cm) cubes.

Add the hummus and boiling water to a large pot. Simmer until the soup thickens and is piping hot.

While the soup is simmering, add the olive oil to a frying pan, and place the pan over low-medium heat. Once the oil is hot, toast the bread cubes until they are an even golden-brown color on all sides and are nice and crispy.

Serve the soup with the croutons, a pinch each of sumac, *pul biber*, paprika and cumin, and garnish with the parsley, black olives and a drizzle of extra virgin olive oil.

Trust me, this ain't no regular beans on toast recipe. These beans become sweet and luscious after simmering in the juices of slowly caramelized onions and tomatoes and are an absolute delight. Do take your time softening both the onions and the tomatoes, as this will make all the difference to the overall quality of the finished dish, as will using creamy jarred white beans instead of canned ones.

Tomatoey Caramelized Onions & Beans (ON TOAST)

ALL IN ONE

SERVES 4
Prep: 5 minutes
Cook: 25–40 minutes
—

3 tbsp extra virgin olive oil
2 yellow onions, peeled, halved and very finely sliced
¾ tsp sea salt flakes
1 tsp paprika
1 tsp *pul biber* (Aleppo pepper/ Turkish red pepper flakes)
1 lb 2 oz (500 g) cherry tomatoes
1 x 1 lb 5 oz (600 g) jar of cooked white beans (haricot/cannellini)
¼ oz (10 g) fresh flat leaf parsley leaves, finely chopped
Juice of ½ lemon + lemon wedges, to serve
½ tsp coarse black pepper
4 thick slices of buttered toast or fresh crusty bread, to serve

Add the extra virgin olive oil to a large frying pan and place on the stovetop over low heat. Once hot, add the onions to the pan and give them a gentle stir, sprinkle in the sea salt flakes, stir again, then let the onions cook down on the lowest heat possible for as long as they need (this could take anywhere from 15–30 minutes) until fully softened and caramelized.

Once the onions have turned jammy, add the paprika and *pul biber* to the pan, followed by the cherry tomatoes, and stir well so that the tomatoes are coated in the onions and spices. Place a lid that is just slightly smaller than the pan on the tomatoes, so that the weight of the lid adds pressure to the tomatoes, allowing them to slowly soften and release their juices for 5–6 minutes.

Once the tomatoes have fully softened, remove the lid, add the beans, stir gently, bring up to a simmer, then add the parsley, lemon juice, and black pepper to the pan. Gently stir, take the pan off the heat and serve the beans immediately, either loaded on top of thick slices of buttered toast, or in bowls with fresh crusty buttered bread, with some lemon wedges for squeezing over.

This is the kind of dish that you'll be grateful you saved the roast chicken carcass for (page 150). I keep backbones from spatchcocked chickens in the freezer to make wibbly-wobbly chicken stocks with or to add to soups like this for extra goodness; if I don't have any on hand, then just using the shelf-stable stock cubes is fine. I usually make this with sweetheart cabbage but feel free to play around with whatever leafy greens you have at home; sweetheart cabbage, kale, green beans, collard greens, long leaf spinach and even frozen spinach all work well.

Chicken, Leek & Pasta Broth

QUICK PREP, SLOW COOK

SERVES 4–6
Prep: 10 minutes
Cook: 45–50 minutes
—

2 chicken or vegetable
   stock cubes, crumbled
8½ cups (2 liters) boiling
   hot water
2 tbsp olive oil
1 lb 10 oz (750 g) chicken thighs,
   on the bone
½ tsp sea salt flakes
2 tbsp butter
1 lb 2 oz (500 g) leeks, washed
   and coarsely chopped
1 lb 2 oz (500 g) potatoes,
   peeled and finely diced
½ tsp coarse black pepper
2 bay leaves
1 leftover roast chicken
   carcass or chicken backbone
   (optional)
9 oz (250 g) fresh leafy greens
   of choice, roughly chopped
5½ oz (150 g) mini dried pasta
   (anelli, ditaloni, ditali
   or macaroni)
1 tsp dried mint
Juice of 1 lemon

In a large jug, whisk the crumbled stock cubes into the boiling water until fully dissolved, and leave to one side.

Rub 1 tablespoon of the olive oil into the chicken thighs and season them all over with the sea salt flakes.

Add the remaining olive oil to a large soup pot and place on the stovetop over low-medium heat. Once the oil is hot, sear the chicken thighs for 2–3 minutes on both sides until golden brown, then transfer them to a plate.

Add the butter to the pot, and once melted, add the leeks, cooking them down for 4–5 minutes until softened. Add the potatoes and coarse black pepper to the pot, stir well, then pop the chicken thighs back into the pot followed by the bay leaves. Add in the leftover chicken carcass or backbone (if using), then pour in the stock and gently stir. Bring everything up to a boil, turn down to medium heat and simmer with the lid on for 30 minutes.

After 30 minutes, carefully transfer the cooked chicken thighs (and carcass or bones) to a plate and add your greens to the pot. Bring the soup back up to a boil (this can take a little longer if using frozen greens), then add the mini pasta shapes to the pot—tiny pasta requires minimal cooking time, so cook for no longer than 5 minutes (without the lid on), stirring when necessary.

Remove the pot from the heat and pop the lid on while you shred the chicken. Remove and discard the skin and bones from the chicken thighs, shred the tender, cooked meat, and add the meat to the soup. Remove the bay leaves. Stir in the dried mint, squeeze in the lemon juice and, if you have time, leave for 20–30 minutes (with the lid on) so that the soup thickens a little more. Feel free to add more salt and black pepper to taste.

EASY MIDWEEK SUPPERS

I can be a bit of an all or nothing cook, either dedicating hours to marinating meats and making homemade bread, or grabbing ingredients to throw a meal together with only 15 minutes to spare. In the week, I need easy meals and these are the faithful recipes I have created over the years.

I love all-in-one cooking methods that make the most of versatile easy-to-cook mince (using whichever option your household prefers best), such as in One-Pot Spiced Beef Linguine (page 76) and Juicy *Köfte* & Spinach Stew (page 92). Or one-pan bakes using flavor-absorbing chicken thighs, such as Pomegranate-Orange Chicken & Potatoes (page 84). Sausages are such a versatile ingredient too and I use them in another all-in-one dish infused with oregano, garlic, parsley and *pul biber* and enriched with cream, All-In-One Creamy Sausage Pasta (page 86). We are huge fans of fish and seafood, turning to quick-cook fillets from the fridge and shrimp from the freezer during the week. I've included our tried-and-tested family go-to recipes, such as the Sticky Salmon & Noodle Bake (page 89), Sea Bass with Herby *Pul Biber* Butter (page 96) and Creamy One-Pan Shrimp (page 90). I've also included one of my absolute favorite salads, a platter of Smoked Salmon, New Potatoes & Lots of Good Green Stuff (page 94), that I make if we have friends coming round on a warm, midweek evening.

After living in London for 37 years, my husband and I decided to move our little family outside of the capital (and perhaps a little out of our comfort zone too), to settle into village life. We were nervous about leaving the accessibility and diversity of city living and not being as close to our wonderful family and friends. Thankfully, we met another excellent bunch of friends who love to host and cook as much as we do. My friend Sarah makes an incredible pasta dish, which she calls, "Hodge Podge" Tuna Spaghetti (page 83), and I have been asking her for the recipe for ages. I was so grateful she shared it with me and allowed me to share it with you too.

Even though the majority of these delicious dishes are quick to put together, I also wanted to give you a couple of tips to make them even more flavorful, if you find yourself with a touch more time:

◉ When making the *Taze Fasulye Yahni* (page 79), and if you have the time, you can start by cooking the onion separately to the other vegetables, adding it to the hot oil first. Take a few extra minutes when softening the onion on low-medium heat so the onion sizzles slowly in the hot oil and caramelizes until soft and jammy, golden brown and slightly crispy at the edges; you really will taste the difference. Fry the carrots, celery and potatoes for a few minutes after you have softened the onion, as the caramelized edges will also impart so much extra flavor to this dish.

◉ When a dish calls for canned chopped tomatoes, please try to use the best-quality chopped tomatoes you can afford. The *Taze Fasulye Yahni* (page 79) and also *Kıymalı Bezelye* (page 80) will benefit from proper good quality canned tomatoes, resulting in a more authentic texture and flavor to the sauce, as if you were using fresh ones. I instinctively opt for finely chopped canned tomatoes as I liken them most to the natural texture of fresh, coarsely-grated ones. Additionally, when tomatoes are deliciously ripe and in season during the summer and early autumn, you can swap out canned ones for fresh.

I have grown up eating pasta cooked directly in the sauce and I adore the way the pasta soaks up the flavor of the juices while it bubbles away. Ensure to gently push long strands of linguine into the sauce as they cook, and stir it as it softens to ensure the strands don't clump together in the sauce or stick to the bottom of the pan. Saucy and delicious, and laden with lashings of grated hellim *(halloumi cheese) and dried mint, this really is a simple, midweek treat. Feel free to swap the linguine for spaghetti.*

One-Pot Spiced Beef Linguine

ALL IN ONE

SERVES 4–6
Prep: 5 minutes
Cook: 30 minutes

——

1 chicken or vegetable
  stock cube, crumbled
3⅓ cups (800 ml) boiling
  hot water
3 tbsp olive oil
1 large onion, peeled and
  finely chopped
¾ tsp sea salt flakes
1 lb 2 oz (500 g) ground beef
4 large garlic cloves,
  finely grated
1 tsp *pul biber* (Aleppo pepper/
  Turkish red pepper flakes)
¼ tsp ground cinnamon
2 tsp dried mint
½ tsp coarse black pepper
2 tbsp *tatlı biber salçası*
  (Turkish sweet/mild
  red pepper paste)
1 x 14 oz (400 g) can
  chopped tomatoes
Scant ½ cup (100 ml) milk
10½ oz (300 g) dried linguine
5½ oz (150 g) *hellim* (halloumi
  cheese), finely grated

In a large jug, whisk the crumbled stock cube into the boiling water until fully dissolved, and leave to one side.

Add the olive oil to a large, deep, nonstick pan and place on the stovetop over medium heat. Once the oil is hot, add the onion to the pan, sprinkle in half of the salt, turn up the heat a little and cook the onion for around 5–6 minutes until it starts to caramelize around the edges. Add the meat, turn the heat up, and break down the meat with the back of a wooden spoon. Stir the onion into the meat, then leave the meat to brown without stirring. After 3–4 minutes, once the underside of the meat is crispy, add the garlic, *pul biber*, ground cinnamon, 1 teaspoon of the dried mint, the coarse black pepper and the remaining sea salt flakes to the pan, and stir well.

Add the *tatlı biber salçası*, stir it well into the meat, add the chopped tomatoes and stir again, leaving the tomatoes to sizzle into the meat for a minute or two. Fill up the empty tomato can with cold water and top up the stock with enough water from the can to bring the liquid in the jug up to 4¼ cups (1 liter).

Pour the stock and the milk into the pan, stir, and once it comes up to the boil, add the linguine to the pan, gently separating the strands into the sauce. Turn the stovetop down to low-medium heat. Keep an eye on the linguine for the first couple of minutes, and once it starts softening, ensure to push down any of the pasta slightly sticking out of the pan into the sauce, continuing to gently swish and separate the strands with a large pair of tongs.

Once the linguine has softened, cook for 10–12 minutes, gently stirring with the tongs every couple of minutes, until the pasta is cooked through but still a little al dente. Serve in large bowls, and sprinkle generously with the *hellim* and remaining dried mint.

I don't know why, but I always find myself making this dish on a Tuesday evening. It's the kind of meal I can prep and throw into a pot without having to think too much about what I'm doing. The vegetables are roughly chopped, the spices are simple, and I use either fresh or frozen green beans to make this—either will suffice. The recipe makes quite a big batch, which can easily be frozen, and tastes even better the next day like most yahni (tomato-based stew) dishes do. It's just as delicious cold as it is hot. I serve it simply with fresh crusty bread or rice, pickled peppers, black olives, raw onion and a dollop of thick plain yogurt. To cook in the slow cooker, see page 205.

Taze Fasulye Yahni GREEN BEAN STEW

ALL IN ONE

SERVES 6 (OR 4 WITH LEFTOVERS FOR THE FRIDGE OR FREEZER)
Prep: 10 minutes
Cook: 45 minutes
—
1 vegetable stock cube, crumbled
1¼ cups (300 ml) boiling hot water
3 tbsp olive oil
1 large yellow onion, peeled and roughly chopped into ½–¾ in (1–2 cm) pieces
3 large carrots, peeled and sliced into ½ in (1 cm) discs
2 celery sticks, roughly sliced, ½ in (1 cm) thick
1 lb 2 oz (500 g) Yukon Gold or Russet potatoes, peeled and cut into 1¼ in (3 cm) chunks
4 garlic cloves, finely grated
1 tbsp tomato paste
2 tbsp *tatlı biber salçası* (Turkish sweet/mild red pepper paste)
½ tsp ground cumin
1 lb 2 oz (500 g) green beans
1 x 14 oz (400 g) can finely chopped tomatoes
½ tsp fine sea salt (salt to taste, depending on how salty your stock is)
½ tsp coarse black pepper
2 bay leaves

In a jug, whisk the crumbled stock cube into the boiling water until fully dissolved, and leave to one side.

Add the olive oil to a large pot and place on the stovetop over medium heat. Once the oil is hot, add the onion, carrots, celery and potatoes to the pot and cook for 5–6 minutes, stirring occasionally, until the edges brown and the onion starts to soften.

Add the garlic to the pot, stir, then add the tomato paste, *tatlı biber salçası* and cumin, and cook the spicy paste down for a couple of minutes until it releases its aroma, while stirring continuously.

Add the green beans to the pot and stir until they are fully coated in the spicy paste. Pour in the chopped tomatoes, stir and let them bubble and reduce down for 3–4 minutes.

Fill up the empty tomato can with cold water and pour it into the jug of stock to bring the liquid up to 2 cups (500 ml).

Season the beans and vegetables with the fine sea salt and coarse black pepper, pour in the stock, throw in the bay leaves, bring everything up to a boil, then turn the heat down and simmer with the lid on for 30 minutes or until reduced but still saucy.

Take the pot off the heat and, if you have time, let it sit with the lid on, for 30 minutes before serving, so that the flavors really come together. Remove the bay leaves before serving. Tastes even better the next day.

My mom has always made this stew with diced lamb shoulder and I included that recipe in my first cookbook, Meliz's Kitchen; *however, my Aunty Revza makes a version with ground lamb that we affectionately call "Peas Dinner." Use any ground meat you like—lamb, beef, chicken and plant-based all work well, but I find lamb to be the most authentic and flavorful. This tastes even better if you make it the day before you want to eat it, lasts for up to 3 days in the fridge, and freezes well. It works well in the slow cooker (just ensure you brown the vegetables and ground meat first for maximum flavor)—see page 206.*

Kıymalı Bezelye PEA & GROUND LAMB STEW
ALL IN ONE

SERVES 4–6
Prep: 10 minutes
Cook: 40–45 minutes
—

1 **chicken stock cube,** crumbled
2½ cups (600 ml) **boiling hot water**
3 tbsp **olive oil**
1 large **yellow onion,** peeled and finely chopped
2 large **carrots,** peeled and sliced into ½ in (1 cm) rounds
4 medium **Yukon Gold or Russet potatoes,** peeled and chopped into 1¼ in (3 cm) chunks
1 lb 2 oz (500 g) **ground lamb**
1 tsp **sea salt flakes**
1 tsp **coarse black pepper**
4 large **garlic cloves,** crushed or finely grated
1 tsp **paprika**
¼ tsp **ground cinnamon**
½ tsp **ground cumin**
5 cups (700 g) **frozen peas**
1 x 14 oz (400 g) can **chopped tomatoes**
2 tbsp *tatlı biber salçası* (Turkish sweet/mild red pepper paste)
1 **bay leaf**

In a jug, whisk the crumbled stock cube into the boiling water until fully dissolved, and leave to one side.

Add the olive oil to a large pot and place on the stovetop over medium heat. Once the oil is hot, add the onion, carrots and potatoes to the pot and cook down the vegetables for 10–12 minutes, until the onion starts to soften and the carrots and potatoes brown along the edges, stirring often.

Turn up the heat, add the ground lamb to the pot, and break it up into the vegetables with the back of a wooden spoon. Season with the sea salt flakes and coarse black pepper, and brown the meat and vegetables for 5–6 minutes, stirring often.

Add the garlic, paprika, cinnamon and cumin to the pot, and stir for a minute or two until the spices release their aroma.

Add the frozen peas, stir well, then add the chopped tomatoes, *tatlı biber salçası*, the stock and bay leaf. Bring up to a boil, turn the heat down slightly and simmer with the lid half on for around 15–20 minutes until the peas are tender and the sauce has thickened but is still juicy.

If you have time, leave to sit for 30 minutes with the lid on before serving so that all the flavors really come together. Remove the bay leaf. Serve with rice or fresh bread (page 191), and thick plain yogurt.

This is my friend Sarah's recipe. It's the kind of recipe that you can easily substitute one ingredient for another: tuna for smoked mackerel, swap the lemons for limes, use whatever green vegetables are in season. I make this with pul biber, *of course.*

"Hodge Podge" Tuna Spaghetti

FAST AND FRESH

SERVES 4–6
Prep: 15 minutes
Cook: 20 minutes

——

2 large unwaxed lemons
4 tbsp extra virgin olive oil
1 tsp coarse black pepper
 + extra to finish
1 tsp *pul biber* (Aleppo pepper/
 Turkish red pepper flakes)
2 tsp sea salt flakes
4 large eggs
10½ oz (300 g) dried spaghetti
 or linguine
7 oz (200 g) fine green beans
3½ oz (100 g) baby spinach
 leaves
2 x 5¾ oz (160 g) cans tuna
 (in spring water), drained
8 canned anchovies in olive oil,
 finely chopped (reserve the oil)
7 oz (200 g) ripe baby plum
 tomatoes, quartered
2 tbsp capers, finely chopped
24 pitted Kalamata olives,
 halved
1 oz (25 g) fresh basil leaves,
 finely chopped
1 oz (25 g) fresh parsley leaves,
 finely chopped

Zest one of the lemons and juice them both to gain about 4 tablespoons of lemon juice in total. In a small jar, combine 2 tablespoons of the lemon juice and all of the lemon zest, the extra virgin olive oil, black pepper, *pul biber* and ¾ teaspoon of the sea salt flakes. Screw the lid on tightly and shake vigorously until the dressing emulsifies. Leave aside.

Place the eggs in a small pan, cover with cold water, bring up to a boil and cook for 5 minutes. Place the pan straight under cold running water so that the eggs stop cooking. Leave to one side.

Bring a large pot of water to a boil over high heat. Add the remaining sea salt, followed by the spaghetti, separating the strands with a large pair of tongs so they don't clump together while cooking. Once the pasta has been cooking for 6–7 minutes, add the green beans to the pot and cook with the pasta for a final 3 minutes until both the spaghetti and green beans are still a little al dente (follow package instructions, but for spaghetti, it's usually no more than 10 minutes).

While the pasta cooks, peel and quarter the eggs. Add the spinach leaves to a large platter, along with half of the quartered eggs, the flaked tuna, a generous drizzle of the anchovy oil, the tomatoes and 2 tablespoons of lemon juice, then lightly toss them together.

Pour the cooked spaghetti and beans into a colander, without draining fully (otherwise the pasta will stick together) and place them back in the pot, which should be fully dry. You need to work quickly, so shake the dressing jar vigorously again, pour half of the dressing into the pot and give the spaghetti a really good swish with a large pair of tongs so that the pasta turns glossy.

Add the anchovies, capers, olives, basil and parsley leaves to the pot, along with the remaining dressing, stir again, then place half of the spaghetti onto the platter of dressed leaves and lightly toss all of the ingredients together before adding the remaining pasta to the platter, gently mixing everything together again. Add the remaining eggs, give everything one final toss, drizzle over a little more of the anchovy oil, season with a little more black pepper, and serve immediately so that the pasta stays warm.

This is a beautifully tasting dish where sweet, zesty, spicy flavors all come together in one pan. The marination process can start the night before to save time on preparation while also maximizing on flavor.

Pomegranate-Orange Chicken & Potatoes

ALL IN ONE

SERVES 4–6
Prep: 10 minutes + chosen marination time
Cook: 30–35 minutes

—

1 small orange
2 tbsp thick plain yogurt
1 tsp *pul biber* (Aleppo pepper/ Turkish red pepper flakes)
    + a little extra for garnish
2 tsp smoked paprika
2 tsp garlic granules
2 tsp dried oregano
1 tbsp runny honey
2 tbsp pomegranate molasses
3 tbsp olive oil
8–10 large boneless, skinless chicken thighs
1 lb 8 oz (700 g) Yukon Gold or Russet potatoes, washed and cut into ¾ in (2 cm) cubes
1 tbsp cornstarch
1½ tsp sea salt flakes
¾ tsp coarse black pepper
¼ cup (10 g) fresh cilantro leaves, finely chopped

Zest the orange and leave the orange whole to use later in the recipe. In a large dish, mix together the orange zest, yogurt, *pul biber*, smoked paprika, garlic granules, dried oregano, honey, pomegranate molasses and 1 tablespoon of the olive oil. Add the chicken thighs to the dish and mix and coat well in the marinade. Cover and refrigerate for at least an hour, or overnight (no longer than 24 hours).

Take the chicken out of the fridge 30 minutes before cooking and preheat the oven to 425°F (220°C).

Brush a large, shallow, nonstick baking pan with 1 tablespoon of the olive oil.

Add the cubed potatoes to the chicken dish. Squeeze out 2 tbsp of juice from the orange. Add the orange juice to the marinated chicken thighs and potatoes, stir well, then sprinkle in the cornstarch, stirring well again, followed by the remaining olive oil, and half of the sea salt and black pepper, stirring well again.

Add the potatoes and chicken thighs to the oiled pan, drizzle 2 tablespoons of the marinade juices over the chicken (discarding the rest) and season with the remaining sea salt flakes and coarse black pepper. Place the pan on the middle rack of the oven and cook for 30–35 minutes, turning the chicken halfway through, then flipping again for the final 10 minutes, until the fillets are juicy all over, caramelized around the edges and the potatoes are tender and cooked through.

Take the pan out of the oven, sprinkle over the chopped cilantro leaves and swish the chicken fillets around in all the juices. Serve immediately so that everything remains hot and juicy, and garnish with a sprinkling of *pul biber*.

This is my quick take on a regularly requested recipe my mother-in-law, Edwina, cooks for my children. Over the years, I've changed a couple of things like cooking everything in one pan for ease, and adding some pul biber *and grated cheese in at the end. For the best, most delicious, results, ensure to use excellent quality sausages (any chunky meat or meat-free sausages work).*

All-In-One Creamy Sausage Pasta

QUICK PREP, SLOW COOK

SERVES 4–6
Prep: 10 minutes
Cook: 35–40 minutes
—

8 large, good quality chunky
    sausages of your choice
2 tbsp olive oil
2 large onions, peeled and
    finely chopped
¼ tsp fine sea salt
4 garlic cloves, finely grated
2 tbsp tomato paste
2 tsp dried oregano
2 x 14 oz (400 g) cans
    chopped tomatoes
1 chicken or vegetable
    stock cube, crumbled
2 cups (500 ml) boiling
    hot water
10½ oz (300 g) dried pasta
    (penne, rigatoni or tortiglioni)
Scant ½ cup (100 ml) heavy
    cream (or plant-based
    equivalent)
½ tsp coarse black pepper
A small handful of fresh flat
    leaf parsley leaves,
    finely chopped
1¾ oz (50 g) grated Parmesan
    or Grana Padano cheese
    (or plant-based equivalent)
½ tsp *pul biber* (Aleppo pepper/
    Turkish red pepper flakes)
A drizzle of extra virgin olive oil

Preheat the oven to 400°F (200°C) and cook the sausages as per package instructions until browned all over and cooked through. While the sausages cook, prepare the sauce.

Add the olive oil to a large, nonstick pot and place on the stovetop over medium heat. Once hot, add the onions, stir, sprinkle in the sea salt, then turn the heat down and soften for 8–10 minutes until translucent and a little caramelized, stirring occasionally.

Add the garlic to the pot, stir for a minute, then add the tomato paste and dried oregano. Stir the tomato paste into the softened onions, then pour in the chopped tomatoes. Turn up the heat and allow the chopped tomatoes to come up to a simmer and reduce just slightly for a couple of minutes.

While the tomatoes simmer, add the crumbled stock cube to a large measuring jug and whisk in the boiling water until fully dissolved. Half-fill the two empty tomato cans with cold water and add enough water to the jug to reach 3¾ cups (900 ml) of liquid.

Add the pasta to the pot and stir well to fully coat the pasta in the tomatoey sauce. Pour in the stock, stir again, bring up to a boil, turn down the heat, put the lid half on the pot, and cook on low-medium heat for 12–15 minutes. Stir occasionally but gently so that the pasta doesn't stick to the bottom of the pot.

Slice the cooked sausages diagonally into 1¼–1½ in (3–4 cm) chunks. Once the pasta is just cooked (al dente), turn the heat right down (this is important so the cream doesn't curdle). Add the sausages to the pot, stir well, and simmer for a couple of minutes before stirring through the cream and coarse black pepper. Sprinkle over the finely chopped parsley, grated cheese, *pul biber* and a drizzle of extra virgin olive oil to serve.

We have a nutritious salmon-based meal at home at least once a week. It's a foolproof way of getting some essential, and flavorful, omega-3 goodness on the dinner table. I use gluten-free buckwheat soba noodles to soak up all those delicious pan juices, but feel free to use any egg or rice noodles, following the packet cooking instructions.

Sticky Salmon & Noodle Bake

FAST AND FILLING

SERVES 4
Prep: 5 minutes
Cook: 25 minutes
—

2 tbsp runny honey
2 tbsp pomegranate molasses
3 tbsp dark soy sauce
1 tbsp olive oil
4 large garlic cloves,
    crushed/finely grated
2 tsp finely grated fresh ginger
1 tsp *pul biber* (Aleppo pepper/
    Turkish red pepper flakes)
    + extra for sprinkling
4 large boneless salmon fillets
    (approx. 4½–5½ oz/
    125–150 g each)
½ tsp fine sea salt
9 oz (250 g) dried noodles
    (of choice)
7 oz (200 g) sugar snap peas
    or snow peas
½ tsp coarse black pepper
2 tsp nigella seeds
2 tsp toasted sesame seeds
1 oz (25 g) fresh cilantro leaves
    and stalks, finely chopped

Preheat the oven to 450°F (230°C). Fully line a large, shallow baking pan with parchment paper. Ensure the paper is larger than the pan so the marinade does not seep onto the pan while the salmon cooks.

In a large, shallow dish, mix together the honey, pomegranate molasses, 2 tablespoons of the soy sauce, the olive oil, garlic, ginger and *pul biber*. Pat dry the salmon fillets with paper towels, then place them into the marinade and coat them fully all over. Leave them in the marinade for 10 minutes while you cook the noodles.

Fill up a large pot with freshly boiled water, add the fine sea salt and bring back up to a boil on the stovetop over medium heat. Add the noodles to the pot and boil for 2 minutes, before adding the sugar snap/snow peas and cooking for a further 2 minutes. Drain the noodles and vegetables in a colander placed under cold running water for a few seconds, to prevent them from overcooking, and leave in the colander to drain.

Add the marinated salmon fillets to the lined baking pan and spoon over the marinade still in the dish. Season the salmon with half of the coarse black pepper and bake on the top rack of the oven for 10–12 minutes until just cooked. Take the pan out of the oven, transfer the salmon to a plate and cover with foil.

Run the noodles and vegetables in the colander under cold water again to loosen and separate the noodles, drain, then add them to the same baking pan you cooked the salmon on, and spread out with a pair of tongs. Sprinkle over the nigella seeds, sesame seeds and remaining coarse black pepper, and give everything a swish to soak up the marinade in the pan. Put the pan back in the oven on the top rack for 3–4 minutes to allow the noodles to heat up.

Take the pan out of the oven, stir through the fresh cilantro and serve the noodles and vegetables on a large platter. Drizzle over the remaining soy sauce, and top with the salmon and a final sprinkling of *pul biber*.

Keep fresh shrimp in the fridge or freezer and you'll always have a meal on the table in no time at all. The trick here is to not overcook the shrimp—work quickly with the stirring and adding of the ingredients, and the entire meal can be cooked and ready in around 15 minutes. Feel free to use chickpeas, butter beans or white beans in this one—they'll all taste delicious when coated in the spicy, creamy, coconut sauce. The stew goes well with the Nutty, Herby Brown Rice & Lentils recipe on page 55, or simply with steamed rice or toasted bread.

Creamy One-Pan Shrimp
FAST AND FILLING

SERVES 4
Prep: 5–10 minutes
Cook: 5 minutes
—

14 oz (400 g) large, raw jumbo
   shrimp, shelled and deveined
3 tbsp olive oil
4 scallions, finely sliced
1 large *kapya biber* (capia
   pepper), red romano or
   red bell pepper, halved
   lengthways, deseeded
   and finely sliced
4 large garlic cloves,
   crushed/finely grated
2 tsp smoked paprika
2 tsp *pul biber* (Aleppo pepper/
   Turkish red pepper flakes)
2 tbsp *tatlı biber salçası*
   (Turkish sweet/mild
   red pepper paste)
1 x 14 oz (400 g) can chickpeas/
   butter beans/white beans
   (8½ oz/240 g drained
   weight), drained and rinsed
1⅔ cups (400 ml) coconut milk
7 oz (200 g) baby spinach
   leaves, roughly chopped
¾ tsp sea salt flakes
½ tsp coarse black pepper
1 oz (30 g) fresh flat leaf parsley
   leaves, finely chopped

Pat the shrimp dry with paper towels.

Add the olive oil to a large, deep frying pan and place on the stovetop over medium-high heat. Once hot, add the scallions and *kapya biber* to the pan and soften for a minute or two before adding the shrimp. Allow the shrimp to sizzle in the pan for a few seconds, then add the garlic, sprinkle in the smoked paprika and *pul biber*, and give everything a quick stir before mixing in the *tatlı biber salçası*.

Add in the chickpeas or beans and give them a quick stir to coat them in all the flavors in the pan, then pour in the coconut milk. Stir well again, load the spinach leaves into the pan, and stir them into the sauce until they soften and wilt.

Take the pan off the heat, season with the sea salt flakes and coarse black pepper, swish through the parsley, and serve immediately.

In Turkish and Turkish-Cypriot cuisine, köfte *is the name given to any ground meatballs or patties, whether they're made with ground meat or pulses/vegetables. How the* köfte *are shaped and whether they are grilled, roasted, fried or stewed can make a big difference in both flavor and texture—try to roll these ones a little smaller in size so you can spoon them up with that juicy, tomatoey spinach in one mouthful. To keep the entire recipe egg-free and/or plant-based, use a plant-based ground meat substitute and the suggested flaxseed egg (page 10) as an egg-replacement binding agent for the* köfte.

Juicy *Köfte* & Spinach Stew
FAST AND FILLING

SERVES 4–6
Prep: 15 minutes
Cook: 25 minutes
——

1 lb 2 oz (500 g) ground beef
   or lamb
Scant 1 cup (100 g) fine fresh
   white breadcrumbs
2 large garlic cloves,
   finely grated
1 oz (25 g) fresh flat leaf parsley
   leaves, finely chopped
2 tsp dried oregano
¼ tsp ground cumin
1 tsp *pul biber* (Aleppo pepper/
   Turkish red pepper flakes)
3 tbsp *tatlı biber salçası*
   (Turkish sweet/mild
   red pepper paste)
1 tsp fine sea salt
¾ tsp coarse black pepper
1 egg
2 tbsp olive oil
1 large onion, peeled and
   very finely diced
4 large, ripe tomatoes,
   halved, coarsely grated with
   the cut or flesh-side down
   or 1 x 14 oz (400 g) can finely
   chopped tomatoes
1 tbsp pomegranate molasses
14 oz (400 g) baby spinach
   leaves or long leaf spinach,
   roughly chopped
1 lemon, halved

Preheat the oven to 425°F (220°C) and line a baking pan with parchment paper.

Mix together the ground meat, breadcrumbs, garlic, parsley, oregano, cumin, *pul biber*, 1 tablespoon of the *tatlı biber salçası*, ½ teaspoon of the fine sea salt, all of the coarse black pepper and egg (or egg replacement) until fully combined. Wet the palms of your hands with cold water to prevent the mixture from sticking to them, and roll into 40 mini balls, then brush each one with a little of the olive oil.

Before cooking the meatballs, start preparing the base for the sauce. Add the remaining olive oil to a large, deep frying pan and place on the stovetop over medium heat. Once hot, add the onion to the pan, sprinkle in the remaining fine sea salt and soften the onion for 5–6 minutes until caramelized and golden. Add the remaining *tatlı biber salçası*, stir into the onion, and cook the paste down for a minute or two until the color of the onion changes to a vibrant orangey-red. Add the tomatoes to the pan and turn up the heat so that they start to bubble and reduce. Stir in the pomegranate molasses, turn down the heat to low and stir the spinach leaves into the sauce. You will not need to add any extra liquid to the pan as the spinach will release a lot of moisture while it cooks.

While the sauce simmers, place the meatballs on the lined baking pan and bake on the middle rack of the oven for 8–10 minutes until golden brown and just cooked through.

Add the cooked *köfte* to the sauce and gently stir to coat them. Put the lid on the pan and simmer for 5 minutes. Squeeze in the lemon juice, remove from the heat and serve with a dollop of thick, plain yogurt, and some fresh crusty bread or rice (see page 121).

A good, dressing-laden potato salad is one of my favorite things in the world EVER, and this salad really is loaded with flavor. It's simple to put together, looks really rather pretty and can be on your table in 30 minutes. You can swap the smoked salmon for another smoked fish such as mackerel or trout, or canned tuna.

Smoked Salmon, New Potatoes & Lots of Good Green Stuff

FAST AND FILLING

SERVES 4–6
Prep: 10 minutes
Cook: 20 minutes
—

For the dressing:
1 large unwaxed lemon
3 tbsp extra virgin olive oil
 + extra for drizzling
1 tbsp pomegranate molasses
2 tsp Dijon mustard
2 tsp dried mint
1 tsp sea salt flakes
¼ tsp coarse black pepper
 + extra to serve

For the salad:
1 lb 2 oz (500 g) new potatoes,
 washed
7 oz (200 g) fine green beans
3½ oz (100 g) baby spinach
 leaves, roughly chopped
2 large scallions,
 finely sliced
1 oz (25 g) fresh flat leaf
 parsley leaves or dill,
 or a mixture of both,
 finely chopped
2 tbsp pumpkin seeds
1 large ripe avocado,
 pitted, peeled and sliced
7 oz (200 g) smoked salmon

Zest the lemon, halve it, then squeeze out 1 tablespoon of juice from one of the halves. Cut the other half in half again and retain for later.

Add the lemon zest, 1 tbsp lemon juice and all the remaining dressing ingredients to a small jar, screw the lid on tightly, and give it a really good shake until the dressing thickens and emulsifies. Shake the jar each time you use or pour the dressing.

Place the potatoes in a large pan of cold water and place on the stovetop over high heat. Bring to a boil and cook for 12–15 minutes (depending on the size of the potatoes) until almost tender, then add the beans to the pan. Once everything comes back up to a boil, cook for another 3 minutes, then drain fully through a colander, ensuring there is no water left in the pan or on the vegetables. Let the vegetables cool just slightly, then cut the potatoes in half to enable the potatoes to soak up more of the dressing.

Place the cooked vegetables back in the dry pan, then pour in half of the dressing, put the lid back on the pan, and give it a really good shake. Take the lid off, add the chopped spinach, scallions, finely chopped fresh herbs, and pumpkin seeds to the pan. Stir well so that the greens start to wilt into the warm potatoes, then pour in the remaining dressing, put the lid back on and give the pan another good shake.

Place everything in the pan onto a large platter, ensuring to scoop out all the deliciousness from the inside of the pan, then stir through the avocado slices. Tear up the smoked salmon and nestle the pieces into and onto the salad. Serve with the lemon wedges reserved from earlier, drizzle over a little more extra virgin olive oil and coarse black pepper to taste. A jar of mayonnaise is optional, but welcomed.

This is such a simple recipe, but sometimes the most simple ones are the hardest ones to get right. To ensure a really crispy skin and "just-cooked flesh," pat the fish fillets dry, score the skin (to prevent the fish from curling while it cooks), and gently push them down, skin-side down first in the hot pan for a nice even cook. This recipe also works beautifully with sea bream fillets.

Sea Bass with Herby *Pul Biber* Butter

FAST AND FILLING

SERVES 4
Prep: 5 minutes
Cook: 10 minutes
—

4 large, boneless sea bass fillets
½ tsp sea salt flakes
¼ tsp coarse black pepper
2 tbsp olive oil
4 tbsp (60 g) unsalted butter
½ tsp finely grated or
    crushed garlic
1 tsp *pul biber* (Aleppo pepper/
    Turkish red pepper flakes)
1 tsp very finely chopped
    fresh parsley leaves
2 tsp very finely chopped
    fresh dill
1 unwaxed lemon, zested and
    juiced, + wedges to serve

Pat the fish fillets dry with paper towels, and, using a very sharp, small knife, lightly score the skin in three places. Season both sides with the sea salt flakes and coarse black pepper.

Add half of the olive oil to a large, shallow frying pan and place over medium heat.

Once the oil is hot, place two of the fish fillets, skin-side down, in the pan. Gently and carefully push down the fish with your fingertips or the back of a fish slice to ensure the skin is flat to the pan—this ensures the fillets crisp up, cook evenly and do not curl at the sides.

Cook the fillets for around 2 minutes on each side (check that the underside of each fillet is crispy and golden brown before flipping over). Transfer the cooked fillets to a warmed plate, add the remaining olive oil to the frying pan and repeat the same cooking process as above with the remaining two fillets.

Once you have removed the final two fillets from the pan, place the pan back on the heat, turn down to low-medium, and add the butter. Once the butter has only just melted, stir in the garlic, soften for a minute or so until it releases its aroma, then sprinkle in the *pul biber*, parsley, dill and the lemon zest and 2 tablespoons of the lemon juice. Heat through for a few seconds before pouring the buttery sauce over the fish to finish. Serve with the Charred Greens & Pantry Beans (page 58) or Nutty, Herby Brown Rice & Lentils (page 55), some lemon wedges and some fresh bread to mop up that garlicky, herby, chile butter.

FRIDAY
FAKEOUT

Whenever I eat the meals from this chapter, I am transported to somewhere warm and familiar: my home from home, *Kıbrıs* (Cyprus). Holiday vibes, comforting aromas that waft through the kitchen, and beautiful mezze plates take me straight to a happy place of family celebrations and togetherness.

Celebrating birthdays and anniversaries with family get-togethers at home were a huge part of my life while growing up, so we rarely got take out or went out for dinner to mark these special occasions. When we did, it was usually to an *Ocakbaşı* (grill restaurant) for the familiar flavors of Turkish cuisine. Aside from ordering our favorite *ızgara* (grilled) dishes from the menu, we'd also order a few *lahmacun* to start our meal with, and they are often one of the first things we go out to eat when visiting our family in North Cyprus too.

Lahmacun are circular or oval-shaped pieces of freshly made, thinly rolled dough topped with a spiced ground lamb mixture (which varies in its combination of ingredients and spices depending on the region it comes from). Once prepared, *lahmacun* are cooked quickly, and at a very high heat, in a traditional clay or wood oven until the topping caramelizes and the edges of the dough crisp up. The cooked *lahmacun* are filled with an onion, sumac and fresh parsley salad, a very generous squeeze of lemon juice and then rolled up and eaten. Heaven.

Lahmacun really are a beautiful labor of love, and since the fakeout experience needs to have an element of the ease associated with the actual take-out experience, I "cheat" with my recipe in this chapter. I use thin, halved layers of pita bread that I top with the traditional spiced meat to make Cheater's *Lahmacun* Pitas (page 105), cutting out the additional time needed when making, proofing and rolling fresh dough. You can use gluten-free pita bread to keep the entire meal gluten free, and plant-based ground meat substitute if you're looking for the perfect Friday night vegetarian fakeout fix.

When I first became a mother, I was adamant that we wouldn't stop eating out. We wanted our children to experience a variety of flavors and cuisines when they were young, and eating out was a great way to do that. But regularly eating in restaurants can be expensive and logistically complicated, so we found ourselves moving more from eating out to eating in, without losing our adventurous spirit when it came to flavor.

I find that getting everyone involved in the cooking encourages kids, especially, to try new things, and sharing the task of cooking makes everyone feel part of the "staying in without missing out" sentiment. For me, the Friday night meal is an "all hands on deck" experience; the collective energy of creating fun, flavorful food together, cooking with our own hands, and sitting down to enjoy an impressive array of colorful dishes that have been prepared in unison. Yes that means a little bit more cleanup than going to a restaurant, of course, but I think it's worth it for the moment. I've included dishes like Tangy Fish Tacos & Tahini Tartare (page 102), a playful twist on the traditional British fish and chips, and Crispy Chicken Wings & Pomegranate Molasses Ketchup (page 106), which always goes over well.

This chapter has some of our favorites, including a simplified take on *Çökertme Kebabı*, Spiced Beef & Fries (page 109) and crowd-pleasing *Köfte* Kebabs & Garlic Sauce (page 114). You can really get into this chapter with the Spiced *Köfte* & Potatoes with Tangy Tahini Yogurt (page 111), Loaded Crunchy, Spicy Ground Beef Wraps (page 117), and Spiced Ground Beef & Rice topped with pomegranate seeds and toasted almonds (page 118), a simple, yet impressive centerpiece dish.

You can make the zingy *Ocakbaşı*-Style Salad (page 122) or the Chunky Crunchy Cheesy *Salata* (page 124) in advance to serve with any of the other recipes in this chapter.

You'll also find delicious mezze dips to decorate the table with before you dive in, including Creamy *Haydari* (page 126), Cheater's *Ezme* (page 129) and "Marinated Olives" Dipping Oil (page 130). I don't mess around with the Smokey Eggplant *Mütebbel* recipe (page 128); I just stick to using the traditional flavors and textures of slowly smoked eggplants to enhance a thick, tangy and creamy garlic tahini yogurt.

This is a fab Friday night fish dinner that's easy to bring together in no time at all; make the simple red cabbage salad, whip up the quick tahini "tartare" sauce, bake the lovely spiced coated fish, and you've got yourselves some seriously delicious tacos. The salad and tartare sauce can be stored in the fridge for up to 3 days, and the fish can also be cooked in the air fryer (see method on page 202).

Tangy Fish Tacos & Tahini Tartare

FAST AND FRESH

SERVES 4
Prep: 20 minutes
Cook: 10 minutes
—

For the red cabbage:
5½ oz (150 g) red cabbage,
   finely shredded
1 tbsp pomegranate molasses
1 tbsp freshly squeezed lime juice

For the tahini tartare:
⅓ cup (75 g) tahini
⅓ cup (75 ml) lime juice
⅓ cup (75 g) mayonnaise
½ tsp coarse black pepper
1 tbsp finely chopped fresh
   cilantro leaves
1 tbsp capers, finely chopped
2 tbsp finely chopped pickles

For the fish:
4 large cod or haddock fillets,
   (7 oz/200 g each)
   skinless and boneless
2 tsp smoked paprika
2 tsp paprika
1 tsp *pul biber* (Aleppo pepper/
   Turkish red pepper flakes),
   + extra to garnish
2 tbsp olive oil
1 tbsp pomegranate molasses
¼ tsp sea salt flakes
¼ tsp coarse black pepper

To serve:
8 corn tortillas
1 large ripe avocado,
   pitted, peeled and sliced
Fresh cilantro, roughly chopped
2 limes, cut into wedges

Preheat the oven to 450°F (230°C). Line a large, shallow baking pan with parchment paper.

Place the finely shredded red cabbage in a bowl and mix in the pomegranate molasses and lime juice. Leave to one side.

Place the tahini and lime juice in a small bowl and whisk together until smooth (don't be alarmed initially, as the dip will look like it's curdled before it turns smooth; be patient). Add the mayonnaise to the bowl, whisk into the tahini until smooth again, then add the remaining tahini tartare ingredients to the bowl and stir until fully combined. Set to one side.

Cut the fish fillets into large, chunky finger-sized pieces (approx. 1¼ x 3¼ in/3 x 8 cm) and pat each piece completely dry with paper towels. Mix the smoked paprika, paprika and *pul biber* together on a large tray or plate, then add the fish fillets to the ground spices and gently roll them around until they are fully coated. Drizzle over the olive oil and pomegranate molasses, roll the fish around again to cover the fillets in the sticky, oily spices, and place them on the lined baking pan. Season the fillets all over with the sea salt flakes and coarse black pepper and bake in the oven for 7–8 minutes, or until the fillets are crispy on the outside and cooked through, yet flaky.

When the fish fillets are almost cooked, put the tortillas into the oven to warm up for the final minute or so, then serve them loaded with the tahini tartare sauce, pickled red cabbage, sliced avocado, the cooked fish fillets and fresh chopped cilantro, and top with a generous squeeze of fresh lime juice and a sprinkling of *pul biber*.

Traditional **lahmacun** *is made up of thinly rolled-out dough, topped with a spiced ground lamb mixture, which varies in its combination of ingredients and spices depending on the region, and then cooked at a very high heat. This version, using pre-made pita breads, and with no rolling involved, satisfies my Friday night fakeout craving in minutes, and you can easily swap in plant-based ground meat substitute if you prefer. You can prepare the topping the night before to save on time, or even freeze it and defrost it in the fridge overnight, ready to use the next day.*

Cheater's *Lahmacun* Pitas

TRADITIONAL RECIPE, CHEATER'S VERSION

SERVES 4–6
(MAKES 12 PITA HALVES)
Prep: 20 minutes
Cook: 10 minutes

—

4 large, ripe tomatoes
2 large onions, peeled
1 large *kapya biber* (capia pepper), red romano or red bell pepper, deseeded, roughly chopped
1 green *çarliston* (charleston) pepper or small green bell pepper, deseeded, roughly chopped
1¾ oz (50 g) fresh flat leaf parsley, roughly chopped
14 oz (400 g) ground lamb or beef
4 large garlic cloves, finely grated
1 tsp ground cumin
1½ tsp paprika
1½ tsp *pul biber* (Aleppo pepper/ Turkish red pepper flakes)
3 tbsp *tatlı biber salçası* (Turkish sweet/mild red pepper paste)
2 tbsp olive oil
1 tsp fine sea salt
1 tsp coarse black pepper
6 large pita breads, sliced open into two flat pieces
2 lemons, quartered
Pickled peppers, to serve (optional)

For the salad:
1 large yellow onion, peeled and very finely sliced
1 oz (25 g) fresh flat leaf parsley leaves, roughly chopped
1 tbsp sumac
1 tbsp extra virgin olive oil
½ tsp sea salt flakes

Preheat the oven to 450°F (230°C). Line two large, shallow baking pans with parchment paper.

Quarter two of the tomatoes and both onions, and blend them together with the red and green peppers and the parsley in a food processor. Place the mixture into a sieve over a large bowl so the excess liquid can drain out for 10 minutes, but do not push down on the mixture—allow the juices to release naturally.

Pour out the excess juices from the bowl (or keep to add to a soup or stew), then transfer the contents of the sieve into the bowl along with the ground meat, garlic, cumin, paprika, *pul biber, tatlı biber salçası,* olive oil, fine sea salt and coarse black pepper and mix together really well. The mixture should be quite smooth and paste-like.

Add enough water to a large, shallow dish so that it comes up ⅛–¼ in (4–5 mm) from the bottom of the dish, and dip each pita half, cut-side down into the water, but only so the cut side dampens.

Lay the softened pita halves, with the dampened insides facing upwards, on the lined baking pans. Evenly spread the meat topping over the insides of each of the 12 pita halves, ensuring to go right to the edges of the bread. Bake in the oven for 5–7 minutes or until the topping starts to caramelize and the meat is just cooked.

While the *lahmacun* cooks, prepare the salad by mixing together the onion, parsley, sumac, extra virgin olive oil and sea salt flakes. Halve and thickly slice the remaining two tomatoes.

Once cooked, top with the onion and parsley salad and lots of freshly squeezed lemon juice. I also like to add sliced tomatoes and pickled peppers (optional), before rolling up and devouring.

I am always torn between whether I prefer a crispy chicken wing to a saucy one, so this recipe covers both. The wings are marinated in a beautiful concoction of spices and condiments for maximum flavor, and the cornstarch results in a deliciously crispy coating to the chicken, perfect for dipping into that spicy, tangy ketchup.

Crispy Chicken Wings & Pomegranate Molasses Ketchup

QUICK PREP, SLOW COOK

SERVES 4-6
Prep: 10 minutes + at least
4 hours marinating time
Cook: 50 minutes
———

2 tbsp plain yogurt
3 tbsp pomegranate molasses
1 tbsp smoked paprika
1 tbsp + 1 tsp *pul biber*
   (Aleppo pepper/Turkish red
   pepper flakes)
1 tbsp dried oregano
1 tbsp garlic granules
1 tbsp onion granules
1½ tsp sea salt flakes
1 tsp coarse black pepper
2 lbs 4 oz (1 kg) chicken wings
3 tbsp olive oil
2 tbsp cornstarch
⅓ cup (75 g) ketchup

To make the marinade, place the yogurt, 1 tablespoon of the pomegranate molasses, the smoked paprika, 1 tablespoon of the *pul biber*, the oregano, garlic granules, onion granules and half of the sea salt flakes and coarse black pepper in a large, shallow dish, and mix it all together well. Place the chicken wings into the dish and give them a really good swish in the marinade, ensuring that the wings are coated all over. Cover the dish with plastic wrap and refrigerate for at least 4 hours, or preferably overnight.

Preheat the oven to 400°F (200°C). Brush a large, shallow, nonstick baking pan with 1 tablespoon of the olive oil and place in the hot oven for 10 minutes.

Take the wings out of the fridge while the oven is preheating, uncover, sprinkle over the cornstarch and mix well. Drizzle over the remaining 2 tablespoons of olive oil and stir well again.

Take the baking pan out of the oven, and lay the chicken wings on it in a single layer, ensuring they are not touching each other. Sprinkle over the remaining sea salt flakes and coarse black pepper, place the pan on the middle rack of the oven and bake the wings for 35–40 minutes, until deliciously crispy.

While the chicken wings are in the oven, prepare the dip by mixing together the remaining 2 tablespoons of pomegranate molasses, 1 teaspoon of *pul biber* and all of the ketchup and serve alongside the cooked crispy wings once cooked.

Crunchy fries, spiced ground beef, garlic yogurt and a sweet tomato sauce all come together in my super simple take on a popular Turkish dish, Çökertme Kebabı. I typically use ground beef instead of the traditional small pieces of marinated fried beef (or veal), and oven-bake thin, crispy fries instead of deep-frying shoestring fries to enable a much easier, homemade, fakeout-friendly version.

Spiced Beef & Fries
TRADITIONAL RECIPE, CHEATER'S VERSION

SERVES 4
Prep: 15 minutes
Cook: 40 minutes
—

For the fries:
4 tbsp olive oil
1 lb 10 oz (750 g) Yukon Gold or
   Russet Potatoes
2 tbsp cornstarch
1 tsp sea salt flakes

For the garlic yogurt:
⅔ cup (150 g) thick plain yogurt
1 tsp finely grated garlic
A pinch of sea salt flakes,
   or to taste

For the spiced beef:
2 tbsp olive oil
1 lb 2 oz (500 g) ground beef
1 tsp finely grated garlic
2 tsp *tatlı biber salçası*
   **(Turkish sweet/mild
   red pepper paste)**
1 tsp *pul biber* **(Aleppo pepper/
   Turkish red pepper flakes)**
   + extra to garnish
1 tsp paprika
½ tsp sea salt flakes
½ tsp coarse black pepper
¼ oz (10 g) fresh flat leaf parsley
   leaves, finely chopped

For the tomato *sos* (sauce):
1 tsp olive oil
1 tbsp *tatlı biber salçası*
   **(Turkish sweet/mild
   red pepper paste)**
1 cup (200 g) finely chopped
   tomatoes
1 tsp *pul biber* **(Aleppo pepper/
   Turkish red pepper flakes)**
A pinch of sea salt flakes and
   coarse black pepper

Preheat the oven to 450°F (230°C).

For the fries, brush a large, shallow, nonstick baking pan with 2 tablespoons of the olive oil. Once the oven is hot, place the pan on the middle rack to heat up for 15 minutes while you prepare the fries and garlic yogurt.

In a small bowl, mix together all of the garlic yogurt ingredients, cover and put in the fridge.

Wash the potatoes, pat them dry and cut into ¼ in (5 mm) width fries. Pat them dry again, then place into a large bowl. Sprinkle over the cornstarch, and stir and shake the bowl gently so the potatoes are fully coated. Add the remaining olive oil to the bowl, gently shake and stir again so that the potatoes are fully coated in the oil. Sprinkle over the sea salt, and shake the bowl again.

Take the baking pan out of the oven and evenly distribute the raw, coated fries into the hot oil, ensuring they are all laying flat and not touching each other; this will ensure that they crisp up on all sides. Return the pan to the oven and bake on the middle rack for 25–30 minutes, turning halfway through once the undersides have crisped up. Place a heatproof dish at the bottom of the oven to keep the spiced beef warm once cooked.

While the fries cook, prepare the spiced beef and tomato *sos* (sauce). To make the spiced beef, add the olive oil to a large frying pan and place on the stovetop over high heat. Once the oil is hot, add the meat, breaking it up thoroughly with the back of a wooden spoon, without stirring—allow the meat to crisp up on the underside for 3–4 minutes before you stir and repeat.

Once the meat has browned and is crispy all over, add the garlic to the pan and stir well for no more than a minute until it releases its aroma, then add the *tatlı biber salçası*, *pul biber*,

Recipe continued overleaf

paprika, sea salt flakes and coarse black pepper to the pan, stir well, again, then carefully add the beef to the preheated dish from the oven. Cover with foil and put back in the oven for 5 minutes while you prepare the tomato sauce (the fries should only need cooking for another 5 minutes at this point too).

Use the same pan you used for the spiced beef to make the tomato sauce. Add the olive oil to the pan and place it on the stovetop over medium heat. Once hot, add the *tatlı biber salçası*, breaking it up into the olive oil with the back of a wooden spoon. Stir in the chopped tomatoes, the *pul biber* and sea salt flakes and coarse black pepper, and once the sauce starts bubbling vigorously, remove the pan from the heat.

To assemble, place the crunchy fries onto a large platter, then spoon over most of the garlic yogurt, followed by the spiced beef, then top with the tomato sauce and a few more dollops of the remaining garlic yogurt. Garnish with the chopped parsley and a sprinkling of *pul biber*, and serve with a salad, or alternatively, load everything into Fluffy *Bidda/Bazlama* Flatbreads (page 187).

This is one of my favorite show-stopper dishes. Not only do the flavors and textures taste absolutely incredible together, the entire dish looks so impressive when brought to the table on a large platter. Although the ingredients list appears lengthy, most of them double up for the potatoes and the köfte; it's just a case of preparing them separately due to the differing cooking times. Another bonus is that everything is cooked in one pan, then served on top of a (pre-made, if you wish) tangy tahini yogurt that stores well in an airtight container in the fridge for up to 4 days.

Spiced *Köfte* & Potatoes with Tangy Tahini Yogurt

TRADITIONAL FLAVORS, NEW RECIPE

SERVES 4–6
Prep: 25 minutes
Cook: 45 minutes

—

For the potatoes:
3 tbsp olive oil
1 lb 2 oz (500 g) baby potatoes
2 tbsp cornstarch
1 tsp ground cumin
1 tsp smoked paprika
1 tsp dried mint
1 tsp *pul biber* (Aleppo pepper/ Turkish red pepper flakes)
¾ tsp sea salt flakes
¼ tsp coarse black pepper

For the *köfte*:
1 lb 2 oz (500 g) beef or ground lamb
Scant 1 cup (100 g) fine fresh white breadcrumbs
1 small onion, peeled and finely chopped
1¾ oz (50 g) fresh flat leaf parsley leaves, finely chopped
1 tsp ground cumin
1 tsp smoked paprika
1 tsp *pul biber* (Aleppo pepper/ Turkish red pepper flakes)
2 tsp dried mint
¾ tsp sea salt
¾ tsp coarse black pepper
1 egg
1 tsp olive oil

Preheat the oven to 425°F (220°C). Brush a large, shallow, nonstick baking pan with 1 tablespoon of olive oil. Place the pan in the oven for 10 minutes while you prepare the potatoes.

Wash and halve the potatoes lengthways, then pat them dry with paper towels. Place them in a large bowl, sprinkle over the cornstarch and mix together with your hands until the potatoes are fully coated.

Drizzle in the remaining olive oil, then the cumin, smoked paprika, dried mint and *pul biber*, and mix everything together with your hands, finally seasoning with the sea salt flakes and coarse black pepper.

Take the pan out of the oven and add the potatoes to the hot oil, all facing cut-side down. Place the pan on the top rack of the oven to roast for 15–20 minutes while you prepare the *köfte*.

Mix together all of the *köfte* ingredients, other than the olive oil, really well with your hands, reserving the olive oil to brush them with, once rolled. Wet your hands with cold water (to prevent the mixture from sticking to them), and roll the *köfte* mixture into 20 even, golf ball-sized balls.

Take the hot pan out of the oven, turn over all the potatoes so that they are now skin-side down, and nestle the *köfte* balls into the spaces in the pan. Brush each *köfte* with the reserved 1 teaspoon of olive oil, then place the pan on the middle rack of the oven for 15 minutes while you prepare the dip and salad.

Continued overleaf

Recipe continued overleaf

Spiced *Köfte* & Potatoes with
Tangy Tahini Yogurt *CONTINUED*

For the dip:
½ cup (150 g) tahini
⅓ cup (75 ml) ice cold water
⅓ cup (75 ml) freshly squeezed
    lemon juice
½ tsp sea salt flakes
⅔ cup (150 g) thick plain yogurt

For the salad:
2 small Lebanese, Persian or
    pickling cucumbers,
    or ⅓ English cucumber
    (deseeded) and sliced
3 ripe tomatoes,
    halved and sliced
1 oz (25 g) fresh flat leaf parsley
    or cilantro, roughly chopped
2 scallions, thinly sliced
2 tsp dried mint
1 tbsp freshly squeezed
    lemon juice
½ tsp sea salt flakes
2 tbsp extra virgin olive oil

To serve:
1 tbsp finely chopped fresh
    flat leaf parsley leaves
1 tbsp extra virgin olive oil
½ tsp dried mint
¼ tsp *pul biber* (Aleppo pepper/
    Turkish red pepper flakes)

In a large bowl, whisk together the tahini, cold water, lemon juice and salt until fully combined and smooth (don't be alarmed; the dip will initially look like it's curdled before it turns smooth; be patient, ensure to use cold water, and you'll get there). Once smooth, whisk in the yogurt and then spread the dip onto a large platter or serving dish (preferably one with a slightly raised edge).

Mix together all the salad ingredients, other than the extra virgin olive oil, in a bowl (you can also prepare your salad vegetables in advance, just don't add the dressing ingredients until you are ready to serve), and leave to one side.

Once the *köfte* and potatoes are cooked, give them a gentle swish in the juices in the pan, then pile them all on top of the plated tahini yogurt dip. Garnish with the chopped parsley, then mix together the extra virgin olive oil, dried mint and *pul biber* to drizzle over.

Drizzle the extra virgin olive oil over the salad, stir well and serve everything with some Fluffy *Bidda/Bazlama* Flatbreads (page 187) or hot, freshly baked Simple Seeded Loaves (page 191).

These köfte *are so juicy and versatile, and my preference is to make them with chicken thighs or ground lamb. The minty, spiced garlic sauce complements them beautifully, and both the sauce and the* köfte *mixture can be made in advance and stored in the fridge overnight; however, don't refrigerate the* köfte *mixture for longer than 24 hours—instead, freeze it, then defrost, and use when required. I bake the* köfte *in the oven, but you can cook them on the BBQ (ensure the grill is hot before you place the* köfte *on, to prevent them from sticking, and brush them with a little olive oil as they cook) or in the air fryer (see method on page 203).*

Köfte Kebabs & Garlic Sauce

TRADITIONAL RECIPE, CHEATER'S VERSION

MAKES 6 *KÖFTE* KEBABS
Prep: 1 hour (plus marinating)
Cook: 20 minutes

—

For the *köfte*:
3 tbsp olive oil
1 lb 2 oz (500 g) boneless, skinless chicken thighs, ground in a food processor, **or 1 lb 2 oz (500 g) ground lamb**
1 red onion, peeled and coarsely grated or finely chopped in a food processor
1 large *kapya biber* (capia pepper), red romano or red bell pepper, halved, deseeded and finely chopped in a food processor
1 oz (30 g) fresh flat leaf parsley, leaves and stalks finely chopped
4 garlic cloves, finely grated
1 tsp *pul biber* (Aleppo pepper/ Turkish red pepper flakes)
1 tsp paprika
1 tsp coarse black pepper
1 tsp sea salt flakes
1 tsp dried mint
2 tbsp *tatlı biber salçası* (Turkish sweet/mild red pepper paste)

For the garlic sauce:
1 tsp finely grated garlic
4 tbsp mayonnaise
½ cup (120 ml) runny plain yogurt
½ tsp finely chopped parsley
1 tsp lemon juice
¼ tsp dried mint
¼ tsp *pul biber* (Aleppo pepper/ Turkish red pepper flakes)
½ tsp sea salt flakes
¼ tsp coarse black pepper

Add 2 tablespoons of the olive oil and all the remaining *köfte* ingredients to a large dish, mix together really well, then refrigerate the mixture for at least an hour, or overnight.

Preheat the oven to 450°F (230°C). Line a large, shallow baking pan with parchment paper.

Take the *köfte* mixture out of the fridge, wet your hands with cold water (so that the mixture doesn't stick to them) and shape into 6 long and even-sized *köfte*, each around 1½ x 7 in (4 x 18 cm) in length, directly on the lined baking pan.

Using two fingers, gently push down to create indents all along the *köfte*, ensuring that the *köfte* keep their overall shape.

Gently brush each *köfte* with the remaining 1 tablespoon of olive oil, and place the pan in the oven on the middle rack for 18–20 minutes, or until the *köfte* are golden brown and cooked through.

While the *köfte* are cooking, prepare your garlic sauce—mix together all the ingredients in a small bowl and refrigerate until ready to serve.

Once the *köfte* are cooked, take them out of the oven and serve immediately with the garlic sauce, some hot and fresh Fluffy *Bidda/Bazlama* Flatbreads (page 187) and any of the salads from this chapter.

Prepare to get messy with these wraps because they are juicy, oozy, crunchy and wholesome, and are a complete flavor explosion in your mouth.

Loaded Crunchy, Spicy Ground Beef Wraps

TRADITIONAL FLAVORS, NEW RECIPE

MAKES 6
Prep: 20 minutes
Cook: 25 minutes

—

3 tbsp olive oil
1 large yellow onion,
  peeled and very finely diced
¾ tsp sea salt flakes
1 tsp *pul biber* (Aleppo pepper/
  Turkish red pepper flakes)
1 tsp ground cumin
1 tsp dried mint
2 tbsp *tatlı biber salçası* (Turkish
  sweet/mild red pepper paste)
1 lb 2 oz (500 g) ground beef
¾ tsp ground black pepper
Scant ½ cup (100 ml) cold water
1 oz (25 g) fresh flat leaf parsley
  leaves, finely chopped
6 large tortilla wraps

For the sour cream sauce:
1 cup (240 ml) sour cream
4½ oz (125 g) *hellim* (halloumi
  cheese), finely grated
½ tsp dried mint

Additional fillings:
5½ oz (150 g) mozzarella
  cheese, grated
Salted tortilla chips
**Cheater's *Ezme* (chile dipping
  sauce, page 129)**
Cucumber, finely sliced on
  the diagonal
Romaine or baby gem lettuce,
  finely shredded

NOTE
*If you're entertaining a crowd
you can prepare these in advance
(including pan-frying), wrap
them tightly in foil, then unwrap
to reheat them in a preheated
oven at 375°F (190°C) for 5–
10 minutes until crisp again and
piping hot inside.*

Add the olive oil to a large, nonstick frying pan and place on the stovetop over medium heat. Add the onion, sprinkle in the sea salt and let the onion soften and caramelize for 3–4 minutes.

Sprinkle in the *pul biber*, cumin and dried mint, stir well, then mix in the *tatlı biber salçası*. Add the beef to the pan, breaking it down into the onion and spices, then stir in the black pepper and leave the meat to brown for 3–4 minutes.

Once the meat has browned, add the cold water to the pan, turn the heat right up and cook for another 3–4 minutes until all the water has evaporated. Stir in the parsley, then pour the spiced beef into a large dish to cool down a little. Carefully give the pan a wipe with paper towels.

Make the sauce by combining the sour cream, *hellim* and mint.

Preheat the oven to 350°F (180°C). Line a large, shallow baking pan with parchment paper.

Place a tortilla wrap on a large plate and spread over ⅙ of the sour cream *hellim* sauce. Sprinkle over some of the mozzarella, ⅙ of the beef, a few tortilla chips, some of the Cheater's *Ezme*, some of the cucumber and shredded lettuce, and a little more mozzarella.

Wrap up the tortilla tightly by folding the closest edge over and away from you, then tuck in the sides and continue to fold away until you have a securely-wrapped and enveloped parcel. Repeat with the remaining 5 tortilla wraps.

Place the large pan from earlier on the stovetop over low-medium heat. Once hot, place two of the wraps, folded-edge down, into the pan (so that the seams seal first and are not susceptible to spill open), then gently push them down with the back of a spatula. Ensure the heat is not too high otherwise the wraps will burn. Once the undersides have browned and are sealed, flip over the wraps and repeat on the other sides. Place the cooked wraps on the lined baking sheet and into the oven to keep warm while you cook the remaining wraps. Pan-fry the wraps as above, then add them to the pan in the oven. Serve hot so the cheese is oozy and the beef is juicy, with a bowl of extra Cheater's *Ezme* to dip into.

Even though the flavors of this recipe remind me of eating out, this is home-cooked simplicity, impressively adorned with a combination of spices and nutty textures, and no one needs to know how easy it is to put together. I regularly make a couple of platters of this when hosting a larger dinner party or family gathering, which makes it perfect for a quick and easy takeout-like treat. Serve this spiced beef on top of the Caramelized Onion & Orzo Basmati Rice on page 121.

Spiced Ground Beef & Rice

QUICK PREP, SLOW COOK

SERVES 4–6
Prep: 5 minutes
Cook: 35 minutes
(not including Caramelized Onion & Orzo Basmati Rice prep/cook time, see page 121)
———

Caramelized Onion & Orzo
   Basmati Rice (see page 121)
3 tbsp olive oil
1 yellow onion, peeled and
   very finely diced
1 tsp sea salt flakes
½ tsp finely grated garlic
2 tsp ground pumpkin pie spice
1 tsp *pul biber* (Aleppo pepper/
   Turkish red pepper flakes)
1 tsp ground cumin
½ tsp ground cinnamon
½ tsp smoked paprika
1 tsp paprika
1 lb 2 oz (500 g) ground beef
½ tsp coarse black pepper
Scant 1 cup (200 ml) cold water
¼ oz (10 g) fresh flat leaf
   parsley leaves, finely chopped
⅔ cup (50 g) toasted sliced
   almonds or pine nuts
½ cup (100 g) pomegranate
   seeds

Make the Caramelized Onion & Orzo Basmati Rice (page 121) and let it rest with the lid on while you cook the spiced beef.

Add the olive oil to a large frying pan and place on the stovetop over low-medium heat. Once hot, add the finely diced onion to the pan, and sprinkle over a good pinch of the sea salt flakes. Soften the onion for 10–12 minutes, turning the heat down if the onion starts to brown too quickly—it should slowly soften and caramelize, hence being diced as finely as possible. Once the onion has softened, add the garlic and stir well, followed by the pumpkin pie spice, *pul biber*, cumin, cinnamon, smoked paprika and paprika. Cook for another minute or two until the aroma intensifies.

Turn up the heat, add the beef to the pan, and break it down using the back of a wooden spoon. Sprinkle in the remaining sea salt and the black pepper, stir well, then let it brown and crisp up for 5–7 minutes, only stirring when and if necessary. Add the water to the pan and cook over high heat for around 10 minutes or until the liquid has fully reduced. Stir in most of the chopped parsley, then take the pan off the heat.

Fluff up the rice with a fork, then serve it all on a large platter, topped with the spiced beef, the remaining chopped parsley, the toasted almonds or pine nuts, pomegranate seeds and a side of Smokey Eggplant *Mütebbel* (page 128) and *Ocakbaşı*-Style Salad (page 122).

So many of the dishes in this book can be served with this delicious rice. Although basmati rice isn't traditionally used in Turkish-Cypriot cuisine, I love using it as a contrast to the more traditional short-grain rice varieties such as baldo *and* osmanlık pirinç *(rice). This recipe is versatile and full of flavor, and you can also swap the orzo out for durum wheat vermicelli, while still following exactly the same method. You can also make it with gluten-free brown rice vermicelli, and I've given you my tips for doing this on pages 51.*

Caramelized Onion & Orzo Basmati Rice

ALL IN ONE

SERVES 4–6
**Prep: 10 minutes
(+ 30 minutes soaking
time for the rice)
Cook: 35–40 minutes**
—

1¼ cups (250 g) basmati rice
1 chicken or vegetable
     stock cube, crumbled
Scant 1 cup (200 ml) boiling
     hot water + ¾ cup (175 ml)
     cold water
2 tbsp olive oil
1 small yellow onion,
     peeled and finely diced
½ tsp fine sea salt
1 tbsp or a large pat
     of unsalted butter
2 oz (60 g) dried orzo
     or risoni pasta

NOTE
*See page 50 for why I fry
the orzo until deep golden.*

Place the rice in a large bowl, fill the bowl up with cold water and gently swish the rice with your hand, being careful not to break up any of the grains. Drain as much water from the bowl as possible without losing any grains down the sink by gently holding back the rice with the palm of your hand, and repeat as many times as necessary until the water runs clear (I usually have to do this 4–5 times at least). Once you're happy, fill the bowl back up with cold water and let the rice soak for 30 minutes.

In a large jug, whisk the crumbled stock cube into the boiling water until fully dissolved, then top the mixture up with the cold water. Leave to one side to cool.

Add the olive oil to a large, deep pot on the stovetop over low-medium heat. Add the diced onion and half of the fine sea salt, then soften for 10–12 minutes or until the onion has caramelized.

While the onions are cooking, gently drain the rice through a sieve, again being careful not to break any of the grains. Leave the rice in the sieve to fully drain over a bowl.

Add the butter to the pot and, once melted, add the orzo or risoni pasta and cook for a few minutes with the caramelized onion until the pasta grains turn a lovely rich, golden-brown color. Remove from the heat. Allow the pot to cool down for a couple of minutes, then add the drained rice to the pot, followed by the stock and the remaining sea salt. Return to the stovetop and place on the smallest burner on the lowest heat.

Give everything a gentle stir, place the lid on the pot and cook for 15–20 minutes until the liquid has been fully absorbed.

Remove the pot from the heat, lightly fluff up the rice with a fork, then let it sit, with the lid on, for 10 minutes before serving.

I'll never forget the first time my little girl tried a salad like this in a local ocakbaşı
(a grill restaurant, sometimes also referred to as a mangal, *the latter of which Turkish
Cypriots also use to describe a domestic BBQ). She was only about two and a half at the
time. We put a spoonful of the salad on her plate and her eyes widened as she slurped up
the long and slippery pomegranate molasses-laden shreds of red cabbage. She pulled the
bowl of salad closer to her and started digging straight in with her fork; none of us got a
taste! I've been making my version of it ever since.*

Ocakbaşı-Style Salad

FAST AND FRESH

SERVES 4–6
Prep: 15 minutes

—

2 tbsp lemon juice
2 tbsp red wine vinegar
 or grape vinegar
9 oz (250 g) red cabbage,
 cored and very finely shredded
1 oz (25 g) fresh flat leaf
 parsley leaves, half finely
 chopped and the other
 half roughly chopped
1 tsp dried mint
½ tsp sea salt flakes
2 tbsp pomegranate molasses
1 small carrot, coarsely grated
 or cut julienne-style
2 large, ripe tomatoes,
 halved, then thickly sliced
1 small red onion, peeled, halved
 and very finely sliced
1 small Lebanese, Persian or
 pickling cucumber, or
 ¼ English cucumber
 (deseeded), finely sliced
3 tbsp extra virgin olive oil
1 heaped tsp sumac

Mix the lemon juice and red wine vinegar or grape vinegar together.

Place the finely shredded red cabbage at the bottom of a large salad bowl with some of the finely chopped parsley. Drizzle over half of the vinegar and lemon mixture, sprinkle over half of the dried mint, ¼ teaspoon of the sea salt flakes and 1 tablespoon of the pomegranate molasses, then gently toss everything together with two forks. Pile on the shredded carrot, tomatoes, red onion, cucumber and the remaining finely chopped parsley leaves, drizzle over the remaining lemon and vinegar dressing, sprinkle with the rest of the dried mint and sea salt, and loosely toss everything on top of the pile together, again with two forks.

Evenly drizzle over the remaining pomegranate molasses, then the extra virgin olive oil, sprinkle over the sumac, and garnish with the roughly chopped parsley leaves. Serve immediately.

This salad has pure vacation vibes written all over it. If you can source Ezine peyniri, *a white cheese from Ezine, in North-Western Turkey, then it really is the best cheese to use in this salad. It's creamy and less crumbly than most brined white cheeses, and has an intense, tangy flavor, and yet, is not overpowering at all. Teamed with rich extra virgin olive oil, fresh and dried herbs, the citrus-y heat of* pul biber, *and the mild acidity of the white wine vinegar lacing the crunchy salad vegetables, this is one salad that brings summery joy in every mouthful.*

Chunky Crunchy Cheesy *Salata*
FAST AND FRESH

SERVES 4–6
Prep: 15 minutes
—

5 tbsp extra virgin olive oil
⅓ cup (50 g) pine nuts
9 oz (250 g) *Ezine peynir/beyaz peynir* (Turkish white cheese) or feta cheese, cut into ¾ in (2 cm) cubes
2 tsp dried mint
1 tsp *pul biber* (Aleppo pepper/ Turkish red pepper flakes)
¼ tsp coarse black pepper
1 unwaxed lemon, finely zested and juiced
3 large, ripe tomatoes, roughly chopped
2 small Lebanese, Persian or pickling cucumbers or ⅓ English cucumber (deseeded), finely diced
1 *kapya biber* (capia pepper), red romano or small red bell pepper, halved, deseeded and thinly sliced into rings
1 Romaine or baby gem lettuce, roughly chopped
¼ oz (10 g) fresh mint leaves, roughly chopped
1 oz (25 g) fresh flat leaf parsley leaves, finely chopped
2 tbsp white wine vinegar or grape vinegar
1 red onion, peeled and finely sliced into rings
1¾ oz (50 g) pitted dry black olives

Add 1 tablespoon of the extra virgin olive oil to a small frying pan and place on the stovetop over low-medium heat. Once hot, fry the pine nuts for a couple of minutes, stirring them frequently until evenly golden brown and glistening, then take the pan off the heat. Set to one side.

In a small bowl, mix together the cubes of white cheese with 2 tablespoons of the extra virgin olive oil, 1 teaspoon of the dried mint, the *pul biber*, black pepper and the lemon zest. Set to one side.

Combine the tomatoes, cucumbers, *kapya biber*, lettuce, fresh mint and parsley in a large bowl and toss together well with 1 tablespoon of the lemon juice and all of the white wine vinegar or grape vinegar. It's important to do this first so that the vinegar and lemon juice do not water down the dressing after you add the oil.

Drizzle the remaining extra virgin olive oil over the salad, toss well, then add the red onion, black olives and pine nuts, and the remaining dried mint and toss again. Add the marinated cubes of white cheese to the salad, gently toss and serve immediately.

I'm a sucker for a creamy mezze dip, and haydari *is up there as one of my favorites; I'm sure it's the reason I love my* cacık *(yogurt, cucumber and garlic mezze dip) so thick and creamy too. Haydari is made by whisking together thick, strained plain yogurt (*süzme yoğurt*) with* beyaz peynir *(Turkish white cheese, although you could use feta if you're struggling to source the former) and then flavoring it with garlic and herbs that have been infused in warm butter. In place of the butter, I like to make mine with olive oil and use the warm herb-infused oil to whisk into and drizzle over the* haydari, *finally topping it with some crunchy walnuts for a very welcome contrast in textures. Now where's that warm loaf of bread?*

Creamy *Haydari*

FAST AND FRESH

SERVES 6–8
Prep: 10 minutes
Cook: 3 minutes
—

3 tbsp extra virgin olive oil
2 tsp dried mint
3½ oz (100 g) *beyaz peynir* (Turkish white cheese) or feta cheese
Scant 1 cup (200 g) thick strained plain yogurt
½ tsp crushed garlic
¼ oz (10 g) fresh dill, finely chopped (optional)
¼ cup (25 g) walnuts, roughly chopped
½ tsp *pul biber* (Aleppo pepper/ Turkish red pepper flakes)

Add the extra virgin olive oil to a small frying pan and place on the stovetop over low heat. Add the dried mint to the warm oil and let it soften for a minute or so until it becomes fragrant. Remove the pan from the heat and allow to cool.

Crumble the white cheese into a medium-sized, deep, flat-bottomed dish, and break it down as much as possible using the back of a fork. Add the yogurt to the dish, followed by most of the minty oil, reserving a little for garnish. Whisk everything together really well, then finally stir in the crushed garlic and chopped dill (if using). Spoon everything onto a serving dish and, using the back of a spoon, make deep, swirling indents towards the center of the dish. Pour the reserved mint oil into the center of the dish so that it forms a lovely pool in the indents, then garnish with the chopped walnuts and *pul biber* and serve.

NOTE
You can make the haydari *in advance and store it in the fridge (minus the toppings) for up to 3 days. Keep the reserved minty oil in a small jar at room temperature and garnish with the walnuts and* pul biber *just before serving.*

Mütebbel, or Mutabal, is made all over the Levant, including Turkish and Turkish-Cypriot cuisine. I like making it a few hours ahead so the flavors really have a chance to come together. I'd suggest serving this, the Creamy Haydari (page 126) and the "Marinated Olives" Dipping Oil (page 130) as a simple make-ahead appetizer for a Friday night fakeout extravaganza (as shown on page 127). And obviously, a basket of hot, fresh bread is an undisputed given.

Smokey Eggplant *Mütebbel*

QUICK PREP, SLOW COOK

SERVES 6–8
Prep: 10 minutes
Cook: 20–30 minutes
(if using gas burner) or
45–50 minutes (if using oven)
—
2 eggplants
Scant ½ cup (100 g) tahini
Generous 1 cup (250 g) thick
  plain yogurt
3 tbsp freshly squeezed
  lemon juice
2 garlic cloves, finely grated
½ tsp sea salt flakes
3 tbsp extra virgin
  olive oil

To garnish:
Toasted pine nuts and/or
  walnuts (see page 124)
Pomegranate seeds
Chopped fresh flat leaf parsley
Pul biber **(Aleppo pepper/**
  Turkish red pepper flakes)

If using a gas burner: Remove the ring from one of the stovetop burners, and line the plate surrounding it with foil. Ensure to keep the burner and ignition exposed, and test to see that the gas ignites. The foil will keep the stovetop clean while the eggplants cook. Do not place the ring back on the burner as the eggplant needs to rest and cook directly on the small round burner plate. Turn the burner on medium heat and place one of the eggplants directly onto the burner plate so that the flames are in contact with the skin. Use a large pair of flameproof tongs to turn the eggplant as it chars and blisters on the underside, and keep repeating until it's fully softened and charred all over. This usually takes 10–15 minutes. Repeat with the second eggplant.

If using an oven: Preheat the oven to 400°F (200°C). Place the eggplants on a shallow, nonstick baking pan and bake on the middle rack of the oven for 45–50 minutes or until the skin turns crispy and the flesh fully softens—use a sharp knife to pierce through the skin of the eggplants and into the flesh—if it goes through with ease and the eggplants deflate slightly, they are ready.

Allow the cooked eggplants to cool a little, then flake and peel off the skin—you can place the eggplants under cold, slowly running water to remove any stubborn pieces of burnt-on skin. Pat dry with paper towels, then chop the softened, mushy flesh into small pieces, place into a large bowl. Add the tahini, yogurt, lemon juice, garlic, salt and half of the extra virgin olive oil to the bowl and mix everything together really well with a fork, or whisk until you have a creamy but textured dip. Pour into a serving dish and drizzle over the remaining extra virgin olive oil, and some, or all, of the additional recommended garnishes: toasted pine nuts and/or walnuts, pomegranate seeds, chopped parsley and *pul biber*.

This is quick, simple deliciousness (photo on page 116), and it goes with pretty much anything and everything savory—I even have it with my breakfast! The "cheat" element stems from the fact that instead of using fresh, seasonal tomatoes and finely chopping all of the ingredients by hand as you traditionally would at home or in an ocakbaşı (grill restaurant), I opt for chopped canned tomatoes and a food processor to do all the hard work instead. This recipe makes a nice big batch that lasts in the fridge for up to 5 days, and can even be frozen in smaller portions for up to 1 month (and simply defrosted in the fridge overnight).

Cheater's *Ezme* CHILE DIPPING SAUCE
FAST AND FRESH

SERVES 8-10
Prep: 5 minutes
—

- **1–2 red or green chiles**
- **1 large onion,** peeled and quartered
- **2 garlic cloves,** finely grated
- **1 oz (25 g) fresh flat leaf parsley leaves and stalks,** roughly chopped
- **1 x 14 oz (400 g) can chopped tomatoes**
- **2 tbsp *tatlı biber salçası* (Turkish sweet/mild red pepper paste)**
- **1 tsp pomegranate molasses**
- **1 tsp dried mint**
- **2 tsp *pul biber* (Aleppo pepper/ Turkish red pepper flakes)**
- **2 tbsp extra virgin olive oil**
- **½ tsp sea salt flakes**
- **A pinch of sugar**

Remove the stalk from one of the chiles and finely chop the flesh, including the seeds.

Add the chile and the rest of the ingredients to a food processor and pulse to the consistency of your liking. Taste the mixture and, if necessary, feel free to add some more chile and an extra pinch of salt flakes, then serve.

This dipping oil is based on my popular marinated olive recipe, which can also be found in Meliz's Kitchen *and is made using predominantly pantry ingredients, except for a couple of fresh herbs and a zesty lemon. I chop all the ingredients as finely as possible to make the most mouthwatering dipping oil (photo on page 127) that is just as addictive dipped into bread as it is spooned over salads and dips like Creamy Haydari (page 126). It can be stored in the fridge for up to 5 days, but ensure to take it out of the fridge at least 30 minutes before serving so that the oil loosens again as it comes back up to room temperature.*

"Marinated Olives" Dipping Oil

FAST AND FRESH

**SERVES 4–6 AS AN
APPETIZER WITH BREAD**
Prep: 15 minutes

—

2¾ oz (75 g) pitted Kalamata
   olives, finely chopped
2¾ oz (75 g) pitted green
   queen olives, finely chopped
1 tsp coriander seeds,
   lightly crushed
2 large garlic cloves,
   finely chopped
1 tbsp finely chopped fresh
   flat leaf parsley
1 tbsp finely chopped fresh
   cilantro
Zest of 1 small unwaxed lemon
1 tbsp pomegranate molasses
1 tbsp balsamic vinegar
⅔ cup (150 ml) extra virgin
   olive oil
2 tsp dried oregano
2 tsp *pul biber* (Aleppo pepper/
   Turkish red pepper flakes)

Mix together all of the ingredients in a medium-sized serving bowl and serve immediately. Alternatively, make in advance and store in a plastic container in the fridge until ready to serve, using the storing and serving suggestions above.

SLOW COOKING

I reserve slow cooking for the weekends. This is when I like to make the kind of recipes that are not attention-seeking in terms of preparation, but may instead need a few hours in the oven. This is the sort of food I like to cook on a lazy Sunday or when we have a few people coming over. In fact, quite a few of the recipes in this chapter can easily be doubled up in quantities and cooked in two dishes or a larger pot—perfect if you're feeding a crowd but don't want to be fretting in the kitchen all day.

One of my favorite meals to make when entertaining is *Lahana Dolması* (Stuffed Savoy Cabbage Leaves, page 137). They take a fraction of the time to roll, compared to vine leaf *dolma*, and rather than cooking them on the stove, I put them in the oven where I can leave them to slowly bubble and caramelize without having to really think about them. These stuffed and rolled cabbage leaves are meat-free, yet so rich and earthy, and are bursting with a complete 360-degree umami experience of sweet, caramelized onions, *tatlı biber salçası* (rich, sweet red pepper paste), sour lemon juice and tart pomegranate molasses, all generously seasoned with a spiced tomatoey stock for them to gently bubble away in. Once they are almost ready, the *dolma* are brushed with a spicy *pul biber* butter, which results in a beautiful caramelized top. It's a feast for the eyes and tastebuds, providing my dinner table with the most glorious-looking centerpiece, and my guests with something really rather special to dig into.

I consider weekends to be the time when we, as a family, are able to take it a little slower, but that doesn't mean I am at leisure to spend all day in my kitchen. Consequently, I've simplified traditional recipes, such as *mantı* (mini meat-filled dumplings), that can usually take hours to make, by using pre-made *yufka* (thin Turkish pastry sheets, perfect for savory *börek*/pastries) and rolling and cutting the dumplings rather than individually shaping them. The thin layers of *yufka* in the *Yufka Mantısı* (page 145) are stuffed with a beautifully spiced chicken *köfte*-style filling, then baked in a buttery, tomatoey chicken stock and served with a garlic yogurt and a minty, *pul biber* butter.

The resulting taste and texture of each mouthful is nothing short of incredible. The sheets of *yufka* crisp up around the edges and on top of the *yufka*, and there is an inevitable crunch to the exterior of the pastry that contrasts with the softer center, the latter texture of which is reminiscent of beautiful homemade *mantı*. I make the *Yufka Mantısı* with chicken and would advise you to do the same, but you could, of course, use ground beef or lamb. In the same way I encourage you to use boneless skinless chicken thighs to make the filling for this recipe (instead of chicken breast, which is more susceptible to dry out), I urge you to use a fattier cut if using a red-meat alternative. For tips on how to make the *Yufka Mantısı* completely plant-based, see the recipe note on page 10.

Comforting slow-cooked soups and stews really are perfect for those lazy weekends, and my mom always uses a whole chicken to make soups and broths with, either boiling it whole, or quartering the chicken before adding it to the pot. However, I opt for large chicken legs in the Creamy Chicken & Vegetable Stew (page 147), since I find that the darker meat on the legs is so succulent here. I've also included a simple, yet flavor-packed, all-in-one roasting pan take on a roast chicken, Whole Chicken Bake (page 150), and one of my most popular recipes ever, *Tavuk Kapama* (One-Pot Chicken & Rice, page 143). Another weekend all-in-one roast to try is the *Fırın Kebabı* (One-Pan Lamb & Potato Roast, page 156).

This chapter showcases how slow, lazy comfort food can also be really rather impressive, and my showstopping Juicy Baked *Köfte* & Vegetables (page 154), Salt Beef & Zingy Coleslaw (page 160), Delicious Beef Short Ribs (page 168) served with Crunchy Herby Roasted Potatoes (page 167), and my *Hellimli* Lasagne (page 159) are all testament to that. Since the very first day I shared my recipes, I made my lifelong love affair with *hellim* pretty clear. My favorite cheese is on show in this splendid baked pasta dish, and I again pair it with its true partner in crime, mint. For that quintessential Cypriot flavor kick, this inseparable pairing is evident in the opulently creamy *hellim* and dried mint béchamel sauce, as well as in the vibrant fresh basil, mint and *hellim* pesto. The spiced cinnamon richness of the meaty Slow-Cooked *Bolonez* (page 153), that I make ahead and use in the lasagne, adds to the luscious texture of the layered pasta as well as enhancing those traditional Cypriot flavors and ingredients even further.

I'm always looking for new ways to improve and perfect the classics, and I have a few tips to ensure my Crunchy Herby Roasted Potatoes (page 167) are faultless, each and every time.

◉ For super crispy potatoes, always use a flat, shallow baking pan (without any ridges in the base). Using a deep pan will create steam, which will, in turn, prevent the potatoes from really crisping up while they cook. Using a flat-bottomed, shallow baking pan will ensure that the hot oil doesn't get lost in any ridges that may be in the base of the pan. The potatoes need to be sitting in as much of the oil as possible while they cook.

◉ Ensure there is a generous amount of smoking hot oil in the pan, so that you can coat the potatoes before putting the pan back in the oven. Coating and turning the potatoes in the hot oil will result in an evenly distributed, rich, golden, crunchy coating to the potatoes once cooked.

◉ Do not roast the potatoes on a very high heat otherwise they'll brown too quickly—to get that beautiful contrast in textures from a crispy exterior and a fluffy inside, cook them at 400°F (200°C) on the middle rack of the oven, turning them after 35–40 minutes and giving them as long as they need for crunchy roasted potato excellence. The timings in the recipe are a useful guide, but feel free to add on a little extra time for that added depth of color and crunch.

Dolma *in Turkish means "to stuff" or "stuffing" and* sarma *means "to roll" or "rolled," but since I've grown up speaking the Turkish-Cypriot dialect (rather than mainland Turkish), I have always called any stuffed and rolled leaf* dolma—*without the* dolma *(the stuffing), they would just be plain rolled leaves, right? Anyway, whatever you call them, I urge you to make these incredible stuffed, rolled savoy cabbage leaves in celebration of their mouthwatering beauty; utterly delicious parceled morsels of meat-free joy. Serve with plain yogurt, fresh bread, olives and pickled peppers.*

Lahana Dolması STUFFED SAVOY CABBAGE LEAVES
TRADITIONAL RECIPE, CHEATER'S VERSION

SERVES 6–8
Prep: 30 minutes
**Cook: 1½ hours (plus
30 minutes standing time)**
—
1 large savoy cabbage
1¾ oz (50 g) fresh flat
    leaf parsley
3 tbsp olive oil
1 large onion, peeled and
    finely chopped
1 tsp sea salt flakes
2 tbsp *tatlı biber salçası*
    (Turkish sweet/mild
    red pepper paste)
3 tbsp tomato paste
¾ cup (150 g) white short-grain
    or pudding rice, washed
    (not soaked) and drained
1 x 14 oz (400 g) can good-
    quality chopped tomatoes
2 tbsp dried mint
1 tbsp pomegranate molasses
¼ cup (60 ml) freshly squeezed
    lemon juice
1 tsp coarse black pepper
1½ tsp *pul biber* (Aleppo
    pepper/Turkish red
    pepper flakes)
1 large tomato, halved
    and thickly sliced
1 chicken or vegetable
    stock cube, crumbled
1⅔ cups (400 ml) boiling
    hot water
Scant 1 cup (200 ml) cold water
2 tbsp unsalted butter

Using a small paring knife, cut off the largest leaves from the base (root end) of the cabbage until you have around 20–22 good-sized whole leaves.

Bring a large pot of water to a boil on the stovetop over high heat and, in two or three batches, blanch the cabbage leaves in the simmering water for 2–3 minutes until they soften and wilt (which will make them easier to roll), then transfer them to a large plate to cool down.

While the blanched cabbage leaves cool down, finely chop the smaller, raw cabbage leaves and the core in a food processor, or very finely dice them with a knife, and leave to one side.

Finely chop the parsley, keeping the stalks and leaves separate from each other.

Add the olive oil to a large frying pan and place on the stovetop over low heat. Once the oil is hot, add the onion to the pan, sprinkle in half of the salt, and soften for 12–15 minutes until lightly caramelized. Add the finely chopped parsley stalks and finely chopped cabbage to the pan, and cook with the onion for 3–4 minutes until they soften and caramelize. Add the *tatlı biber salçası* and 2 tablespoons of the tomato paste to the pan, stirring well. Stir in the rice and pour in the chopped tomatoes. Allow the tomatoes to bubble and reduce for a couple of minutes, then turn off the heat and carefully transfer everything from the pan to a large dish to cool down for a few minutes.

Preheat the oven to 400°F (200°C).

Once cooled, add the remaining sea salt flakes, the dried mint, finely chopped parsley leaves, pomegranate molasses, lemon

Recipe continued overleaf

juice, black pepper and 1 teaspoon of the *pul biber* to the rice mixture. Mix everything together well.

Place a cabbage leaf on a large plate, with the widest part (stem pointing downwards) closest to you. Place a large spoonful (around 2–3 tbsp, depending on the size of the leaf) of the filling along the widest part closest to you, leaving the perimeter around the edges free of the mixture. Tuck in the sides, then the top of the leaf over the filling, before rolling it away from you. Place the stuffed and rolled cabbage leaf into a large Dutch oven or lidded roasting pan (around 11 in/28 cm in diameter if round, or 9½ x 12 in/24 x 30 cm if rectangular, 4 in/10 cm deep) with the seam facing downwards (to prevent the *dolma* from opening up while cooking). Repeat until all the leaves and filling are used up, and all the *dolma* are lined up in the pan. Scatter the tomato slices on top of the *dolma*.

In a large jug, whisk the crumbled stock cube and remaining 1 tablespoon of tomato paste into the boiling water until fully dissolved. Whisk in the cold water, then pour all of the liquid into the pan. Cut out a sheet of parchment paper large enough to tuck into the sides of the pan, lay it on top of the stuffed leaves, followed by a dinner plate/side plate (or two) to weigh everything down a little. Cover the pan with the lid (or wrap very tightly with foil), then cook on the middle rack of the oven for 1 hour.

Remove the dish or pan from the oven and place it on a flat, heatproof surface. Very carefully remove the lid/foil, the plate(s) and the parchment paper. Turn the heat up to 425°F (220°C) and put the pan back in the oven, uncovered, on the middle rack for another 20 minutes.

Add the butter to a small frying pan and place on the stovetop over low-medium heat. As soon as the butter melts, sir in the remaining ½ teaspoon of *pul biber* and take off the heat.

Take the pan out of the oven again, brush everything with a little of the melted *pul biber* better and put back in the oven for a final 10 minutes. Take the dish out, pour over the remaining melted chile butter and allow to rest, with the lid/foil on, for at least 30 minutes before serving. Also perfect served with garlic yogurt (page 109) and *Ocakbaşı*-Style Salad (page 122).

Flavorful fried and crispy vegetables are known as **Sebze Kızartması** *or simply* Kızartma. Kızartma *means "to fry" or "frying," but since these vegetables are oven baked, the crispy texture is achieved with a spicy cornstarch coating. The vegetables are elevated with the chilled yogurt and an utterly delicious sweet, tangy and garlicky pomegranate molasses garlic sauce, and I promise you that this dish will convert anyone with a vegetable aversion to fall in love with everything on this platter.*

Fırında Sebze Kızartması CRISPY OVEN-ROASTED VEGETABLES
TRADITIONAL FLAVORS, NEW RECIPE

SERVES 6
Prep: 25 minutes
Cook: 1 hour
—

For the vegetables:
6 tbsp olive oil
4 tbsp cornstarch
2 tsp dried oregano
2 tsp garlic granules
2 tsp paprika
1 tsp coarse black pepper
2 medium baking potatoes,
    sliced into ½ in (1½ cm) rounds
2 medium eggplants, cut into
    1¼ x 2½ in (3 x 6 cm) batons
2 onions, peeled and cut into
    4 wedges (the root still intact
    to hold the layers together)
1½ tsp sea salt flakes
2 large zucchinis, cut into
    1¼ x 2½ in (3 x 6 cm) batons
2 *kapya biber* (capia peppers),
    red romano or small red bell
    peppers, halved, deseeded
    and cut into 1¼ x 2½ in
    (3 x 6 cm) pieces
½ cup (100 g) thick plain yogurt
1 oz (25 g) fresh flat leaf
    parsley leaves
1 tsp dried mint
1 tsp *pul biber* (Aleppo pepper/
    Turkish red pepper flakes)
1 lemon, cut into 4 wedges

Preheat the oven to 425°F (220°C).

Brush 2 large, shallow, nonstick baking pans with 1 tablespoon of the olive oil each, and once the oven is hot, put the pans in the oven for 10–15 minutes while you get the vegetables ready.

Mix together the cornstarch, oregano, garlic granules, paprika and coarse black pepper.

Place the sliced potatoes into a large bowl and sprinkle over a quarter of the spiced cornstarch mixture, coating the potatoes fully, using your hands to mix them and shaking the bowl around. Drizzle over 1 tablespoon of olive oil and shake the bowl again, so that the cornstarch and oil come together to form a paste.

Combine the eggplant spears and onions in another bowl and follow the same method and quantities as for the potatoes.

Once the oiled pans are hot, take one of the pans out and carefully lay the potatoes, eggplants and onions on it, ensuring the vegetables are all laying flat (to ensure a crispy, even cook). Season the vegetables with half of the sea salt flakes, put the pan back into the oven, near the top but not on the very top rack, for 20 minutes while you prepare the remaining vegetables.

Pop the zucchini spears into the bowl you used for the potatoes and follow the same process as above—one-quarter of the cornstarch mixture and 1 tbsp olive oil.

Put the *kapya biber* into the bowl you used for the eggplants and onions, and repeat the cornstarch and olive oil process.

Continued overleaf

Recipe continued overleaf

**For the Garlicky Tomato
& Pomegranate *Sos* (sauce):**
1 tbsp olive oil
6 garlic cloves, **ground down
to a paste**
1 x 14 oz (400 g) can finely
chopped tomatoes or
4 large over-ripe tomatoes,
halved and coarsely grated,
skins discarded
1 heaped tbsp *tatlı biber
salçası* (Turkish sweet/mild
red pepper paste)
1 tsp confectioners' sugar
2 tbsp pomegranate molasses
Sea salt flakes
Lemon wedges, **to serve**

Once the potatoes, eggplants and onions have been roasting for 20 minutes, take the pan out, flip the vegetables over and put the pan back into the oven. Take the other oiled pan out of the oven, and carefully and evenly lay the zucchinis and *kapya biber* on it. Season the vegetables with a good pinch of the sea salt flakes, put the pan back into the oven (beneath the pan with the potatoes, eggplants and onion) and cook for 20 minutes while you prepare the garlicky tomato and pomegranate *sos* (sauce).

Add the olive oil to a nonstick frying pan and place on the stovetop over low heat. Once the oil is hot, add the garlic to the pan and soften for no longer than a minute, ensuring that the garlic does not color. Add the tomatoes, give them a good stir into the garlic, turn the heat up just slightly, then add the *tatlı biber salçası* and confectioners' sugar to the pan and stir really well so they both dissolve into the tomato juices. Add the pomegranate molasses, stir well again and let the *sos* reduce and thicken for a couple of minutes. Season with another good pinch of sea salt flakes and take the pan off the heat.

After the potatoes, eggplants and onion have been cooking for around 40 minutes in total, take them out of the oven, turn the oven up to 450°F (230°C) and place the zucchinis and *kapya biber* on a higher rack in the oven for a further 5–10 minutes so that the zucchinis caramelize a little more (the *kapya biber* won't be crispy, but will be "jammier" in texture). Transfer the crispy potatoes, eggplants and onions to a large platter. Once ready, take the zucchinis and *kapya biber* out of the oven and serve them on the same platter, spooning over dollops of the *sos* (sauce) and yogurt. Sprinkle over the fresh parsley, dried mint and *pul biber* and serve with the lemon wedges. Serve simply with crusty bread.

This is one of my most popular recipes, and I adore seeing the remakes being shared online. The flavors of the stock infuse the chicken, as does the chicken marinade into the rice, so it's a total win-win situation with a simple method and lip-smackingly good flavors at its core.

Tavuk Kapama ONE-POT CHICKEN & RICE
ALL IN ONE

SERVES 4–6
Prep: 15 minutes
Cook: 1½ hours
—

1¼ cups (250 g) parboiled long-grain white rice
3 tbsp olive oil
1 tsp *pul biber* (Aleppo pepper/ Turkish red pepper flakes)
1 tsp smoked paprika
1 tsp dried oregano
¼ tsp ground cumin
2 tbsp *tatlı biber salçası* (Turkish sweet/mild red pepper paste)
2 yellow onions, peeled and quartered
1 large red, green, orange or yellow pepper, deseeded and roughly chopped
6 garlic cloves, peeled and bashed
8 large, bone-in chicken thighs
1 tsp sea salt flakes
¾ tsp coarse black pepper
1 chicken stock cube
2½ cups (600 ml) boiling hot water
¾ cup (100 g) frozen peas
3 bay leaves
1 unwaxed lemon, cut into 6 wedges
2 tomatoes, halved and thickly sliced

To garnish:
Finely chopped fresh flat leaf parsley

Preheat the oven to 400°F (200°C).

Wash the rice, in a sieve, under cold running water until the water runs clear, then leave over a bowl to drain.

In a small jug, create a spice paste by mixing together most of the olive oil, the *pul biber*, smoked paprika, oregano, cumin and *tatlı biber salçası*. Leave to one side.

Add the remaining olive oil to a deep roasting pan or lidded casserole dish and add the onions, pepper and garlic cloves, along with ⅔ of the spice paste. Trim off any excess fat from the chicken thighs. Add the chicken to the pan/dish and give them a good coating in the spice paste, evenly spreading out the chicken, onions and garlic for optimal cooking. Season the chicken thighs well with most of the sea salt flakes and coarse black pepper and turn them skin-side up in the pan/dish. Pop the pan/dish in the oven on the middle rack for 30–35 minutes so the chicken starts to brown and crisp up.

Add the stock cube to the jug with the remaining spice paste, top up with the boiling water and whisk until dissolved.

Once the chicken thighs have browned a little, take the pan/dish out of the oven and transfer the chicken (temporarily) to a plate.

Add the washed, drained rice and the peas to the pan/dish and stir them into the juices. Pour the stock mixture into the pan/dish then put the chicken thighs back into the pan/dish, including any resting juices, on top of the rice, skin-side up. Add in the bay leaves, lemon wedges and tomato slices, season the tomatoes with the remaining sea salt flakes and coarse black pepper and put the pan/dish back on the middle rack of the oven, turning the heat up to 410°F (210°C). Bake for 30–35 minutes, until the rice is cooked through—it should be juicy and not dried out.

Remove from the oven and let it rest, covered with foil or with the lid on for 10 minutes or so, for the rice soak up the remaining juices. Remove the bay leaves. Garnish with chopped parsley.

I know this one looks long but it's actually a simpler, quicker and less technical version of homemade mantı *(stuffed dumplings). The crispy, baked edges of the filo crisp up like* börek *(filled pastries) providing an inevitable crunch, which contrasts with the softer center reminiscent of* mantı. *If you are unable to source traditional* yufka, *then use two large sheets of filo pastry for each halved (semi-circular) sheet of* yufka, *brushing one filo sheet with melted butter before placing the other on top.*

Yufka Mantısı BAKED FILO DUMPLINGS
TRADITIONAL RECIPE, CHEATER'S VERSION

SERVES 4–6
Prep: 30 minutes
Cook: 1 hour
—

For the stock:
½ **chicken stock cube,** crumbled
1¼ **cups (300 ml) boiling
    hot water**
1 **tbsp olive oil**
1 **tbsp unsalted butter**
1 **tbsp** *tatlı biber salçası*
    **(Turkish sweet/mild
    red pepper paste)**

For the filling:
1 **large onion,** peeled, chopped
1 **oz (30 g) fresh flat leaf parsley,**
    roughly chopped
1 **lb 2 oz (500 g) skinless and
    boneless chicken thighs,**
    cut into bite-sized chunks
4 **large garlic cloves,**
    finely grated
1 **tsp dried mint**
1 **tsp ground cumin**
½ **tsp ground cinnamon**
1 **tsp paprika**
1 **tsp** *pul biber* **(Aleppo pepper/
    Turkish red pepper flakes)**
¾ **tsp ground black pepper**
¾ **tsp sea salt flakes**
1 **tbsp olive oil**
1 **tbsp thick plain yogurt**
1 **tbsp** *tatlı biber salçası*
    **(Turkish sweet/mild
    red pepper paste)**

Continued overleaf

In a jug, whisk the crumbled stock cube into the boiling water, and once dissolved, leave to one side.

For the filling, blend the onion and parsley in a food processor or chop them as finely as possible (for a smoother-textured filling), then squeeze them through a sieve so that any excess moisture is released. Add the onion and parsley to a large bowl.

Blitz the chicken in the food processor until its texture is almost that of ground meat. Add the chicken to the bowl with the onion and parsley, along with the rest of the filling ingredients and mix everything together well. Leave to one side.

Preheat the oven to 400°F (200°C).

Fold the large, circular *yufka* sheets in half and cut across the middle so that you are left with 6 semi-circles. Place the straight edge of one of the semi-circular sheets of *yufka* closest to you. If using regular filo pastry, lay one rectangular sheet in front of you horizontally, brush with a little of the melted butter, then place another sheet on top. Whether you are using *yufka* or filo, ensure to cover the remaining sheets with clean tea towels to prevent them from drying out.

Lay one-fifth of the chicken filling mixture all along the bottom of the long, straight edge of the pastry closest to you, around ¾ in (2 cm) in from the edges. Tuck in the sides of the pastry, then roll all the way down from the top until you have one long pastry filled sausage. Repeat with the rest of the mixture and the remaining 4 sheets of pastry (if using *yufka*, you can freeze the final semi-circular sheet of pastry for another time to avoid any food wastage.)

Line the pastry rolls horizontally and cut through all 5 rolls together, at roughly 2 in (5 cm) intervals, until you have around 40–50 pieces in total, depending on the length of your pastry rolls.

Recipe continued overleaf

For the *mantı*:
3 large sheets of large, circular *yufka* (usually 29½–31½ in/75–80 cm in diameter) or 10 large sheets of filo pastry
2 tbsp unsalted butter, melted
1 tsp olive oil

For the garlic yogurt:
⅔ cup (150 g) plain yogurt (it doesn't have to be thick-set as it will be poured over)
1 tsp finely grated or crushed garlic
A pinch of sea salt flakes, or to taste

For the chile butter:
3½ tbsp unsalted butter
2 tbsp olive oil
1 tsp *tatlı biber salçası* (Turkish sweet/mild red pepper paste)
1 tsp *pul biber* (Aleppo pepper/ Turkish red pepper flakes)
½ tsp dried mint

To garnish:
¼ tsp sumac
½ tsp *pul biber* (Aleppo pepper/ Turkish red pepper flakes)
1 oz (25 g) fresh flat leaf parsley leaves, finely chopped

NOTE
If using plant-based ground meat substitute and vegetable stock, you could also use a plant-based yogurt and a plant-based butter to make it completely plant-based.

Line a small, deep ovensafe pan or casserole dish (roughly 9½ in/ 24 cm in diameter, if round, or 8½ x 8½ in/22 x 22 cm if square, and 8 x 9½ in/20 x 24 cm if rectangular) with an oversized piece of parchment paper that hangs over the edges of the dish (if you wish, you can use the parchment paper to lift the *yufka mantısı* out of the dish once cooked). Brush the parchment paper with the olive oil, then vertically line up the *yufka mantısı* in the pan/dish, ensuring they are nice and snug.

Brush the tops of the *yufka mantısı* with the remaining melted butter, then place the dish on the bottom rack of the oven and bake for 30–35 minutes until the tops of the pastry are lightly golden.

While the *yufka mantısı* cook, prepare the other elements.

To make the garlic yogurt, mix together the yogurt and garlic in a small bowl, add a pinch of salt to taste, then put it in the fridge.

To finish the stock, add the olive oil and butter to a pan and place on the stovetop over medium heat. Once the butter has melted, whisk in the *tatlı biber salçası*, then pour in the pre-prepared stock from earlier. Turn up the heat so the mixture starts to bubble vigorously, then turn the heat down a little and let it reduce and thicken by about a quarter. Remove the pan from the heat.

After the *yufka mantısı* have been in the oven for 30–35 minutes, carefully take out the pan/dish and pour the stock mixture evenly over the top of the crispy pastry. Pop the pan/dish back in the oven, this time on the middle rack, for another 15–20 minutes.

Take the *yufka mantısı* out of the oven and place the pan/dish on a heatproof surface. To prepare the chile butter, use the same pan you used for the tomatoey stock (give the pan a little wash/ wipe first. Melt the butter in the pan on the stovetop over medium heat, then add the olive oil. Once it starts to sizzle, stir through the *tatlı biber salçası*, *pul biber* and dried mint. Once it starts to bubble, remove the pan from the heat.

Liberally drizzle the garlic yogurt on top of the *yufka mantısı*, followed by the chile butter, and finish off with a sprinkling of sumac, *pul biber* and finely chopped flat leaf parsley. Then serve.

Recipes like this really do benefit from using free-range or organic chicken for maximum flavor. This recipe is for chicken legs, but you could use chicken thighs. You could also use skinless and boneless chicken thighs, shredding the tender meat into the stew once cooked. The creamy texture of this stew comes from the terbiye—*a thickening agent made from mixing together an egg yolk, flour, yogurt and lemon juice. Take your time with this one—we're in no hurry, remember. Make it for a lazy Sunday supper and enjoy the warming, hearty leftovers on a Monday.*

Creamy Chicken & Vegetable Stew

ALL IN ONE

SERVES 4–6
Prep: 15 minutes
Cook: 1 hour 20 minutes
——

2 chicken stock cubes
7⅔ cups (1.8 liters)
   boiling hot water
4 large chicken legs,
   skin-on
1 tsp sea salt flakes + a little
   extra for garnish
3 tbsp olive oil
4 large potatoes,
   peeled and quartered
4 large carrots, peeled
   and halved
4 onions, peeled and quartered
2 large celery sticks, quartered
1 tsp coarse black pepper
   + a little extra for garnish
1 tsp paprika
1 tsp *pul biber* (Aleppo pepper/
   Turkish red pepper flakes)
   + a little extra for garnish
½ tsp dried mint
1 tsp dried oregano
1 large egg yolk
1 heaped tbsp all-purpose flour
1 heaped tbsp plain yogurt
Juice of 1 lemon, + extra lemon
   wedges to serve
⅓ cup (60 g) short-grain
   white rice, washed
   and drained
1 oz (25 g) fresh parsley leaves,
   finely chopped + a little extra
   for garnish

In a jug, whisk the stock cubes into the boiling water until fully dissolved. Season the chicken liberally all over with the sea salt.

Add the olive oil to a large soup pot or Dutch oven and place on the stovetop over medium heat. Once hot, add the chicken to the pot, skin-side down, and brown for 2–3 minutes on each side until golden brown. Transfer the chicken to a plate.

Add the potatoes, carrots, onions and celery to the pot and brown for a couple of minutes. Add the coarse black pepper, paprika, *pul biber*, dried mint and dried oregano to the vegetables, stir well, and cook for another 4–5 minutes, stirring often, then transfer the vegetables to another plate.

Place the pot back on the stovetop over medium heat, and pour in the stock. Using a wooden spoon, scrape up any delicious bits stuck to the base of the pot, so they disperse into the stock— this process is known as "deglazing." Put the seared chicken back in. Bring the stock up to a boil, skim off any foam from the top of the simmering stock and discard. Simmer the chicken, half-covered with a lid, on low heat for 45 minutes.

Whisk together the egg yolk, flour, yogurt and lemon juice until completely smooth. This mixture is known as the *terbiye*.

Once the chicken legs have been simmering for 45 minutes, return the seared vegetables to the pot, along with the rice, and give everything a stir. Bring up to a low simmer and cook the vegetables for 15 minutes. If you feel the broth could do with a little more liquid, then top up with a scant 1 cup (200 ml) of boiling water. The broth should thicken when you add in the *terbiye*.

Recipe continued overleaf

Creamy Chicken & Vegetable Stew *CONTINUED*

Using a ladle, take a large spoonful of the stock out of the pot and into the bowl with the *terbiye* and whisk together very quickly. This will temper the *terbiye* so it doesn't curdle when you add it to the soup. Add the tempered *terbiye*, a spoonful at a time, into the pot, quickly stirring it in as you do so that the stock stays completely smooth, and keep repeating until all of the *terbiye* has been added. The stock will now have a creamier consistency. Keep simmering the stew on low heat for another 5 minutes, then stir in the chopped parsley just before serving.

Season with sea salt flakes and coarse black pepper, to taste if necessary, and a sprinkling of *pul biber*, more chopped parsley and a generous extra squeeze of lemon juice to serve.

This mouthwatering whole chicken one-pan bake is a fantastic, simpler alternative for a roast chicken dinner, and tastes even better in the summer when fresh tomatoes are at their best. It's a great one to make when entertaining a crowd; simply double up the recipe, put two pans in the oven and in an hour and a half your guests will be digging into crispy chicken skin, succulent meat, buttery potatoes and a delicious garlicky, tomatoey gravy from the bottom of the pans.

Whole Chicken Bake

ALL IN ONE

SERVES 4-6
Prep: 15 minutes
Cook: 1 hour 30 minutes

—

1 large whole chicken
  (approx 4 lb 8 oz/2 kg)
3 tbsp olive oil
4 large onions, peeled and
  thickly sliced into ½ in (1 cm)
  rounds
1¼ tsp sea salt flakes
1 chicken stock cube
1¼ cups (300 ml) boiling
  hot water
6 large Cyprus, Russet
  or Yukon Gold potatoes,
  peeled and quartered
10 garlic cloves,
  peeled and left whole
A few sprigs of fresh rosemary
A few sprigs of fresh thyme
2 bay leaves
1 unwaxed lemon, finely zested,
  then cut into 6 wedges
½ tsp coarse black pepper
2 tsp dried oregano
14 oz (400 g) cherry or
  baby plum tomatoes,
  preferably on the vine

Preheat the oven to 475°F (240°C). Remove the chicken from the fridge 30 minutes before cooking to bring up to room temperature.

Brush a large roasting pan with 1 tablespoon of the olive oil and add the onion slices to the pan, coating them in the oil then placing them in the center of the pan to work as a trivet for the chicken. Place the chicken on top of the onions and drizzle over 2 tablespoons of olive oil, coating the skin and the underside of the bird and seasoning with 1 teaspoon of the sea salt flakes all over. Place the pan on the middle rack of the oven for 20 minutes for the skin to brown a little. While the chicken cooks, whisk the stock cube into a jug of the boiling water, and leave to one side.

After the chicken has been roasting for 20 minutes, take the pan out of the oven and turn the heat down to 400°F (200°C). Add the potatoes, garlic, rosemary, thyme, bay leaves, lemon zest and wedges to the pan, turning them over in the hot oil, then season them with the remaining sea salt flakes, coarse black pepper and oregano. Carefully pour in the stock, then place the pan back in the oven on the middle rack to cook for another 40 minutes, before adding the tomatoes to the pan and returning to the oven for another 15–20 minutes.

Take the pan out of the oven, check that the chicken is cooked (use a food thermometer or gently tug at one of the legs—the thickest part of the chicken should reach 167°F (75°C) and the juices should run clear), then transfer the chicken to a board covered with foil to rest for 10 minutes. Put the pan back in the oven for 10 minutes while the chicken rests so that the vegetables stay hot and caramelize a little more. Remove the bay leaves. Carve the chicken and arrange with the vegetables on a platter, spooning over the pan juices before serving.

I simply love the fact that the literal phonetic Turkish translation for an Italian Bolognese is Bolonez. *I must add that this is certainly not a traditional recipe for Bolognese; the roots of it perhaps lie more in a rich, tomatoey ragù, while utilizing ingredients such as pomegranate molasses and cinnamon, flavors synonymous with my own Turkish-Cypriot traditions. This recipe easily serves 12 hungry people, so feel free to freeze it in smaller batches to suit your household. If you'd prefer to leave out the wine, just add a little of the stock at the point where you'd add the wine and let it reduce down into the meat for the flavors to intensify.*

Slow-Cooked *Bolonez*

QUICK PREP, SLOW COOK

MAKES 12 (GENEROUSLY)
Prep: 15 minutes
Cook: 2–3½ hours
——
1 beef stock cube, crumbled
1⅔ cups (400 ml) boiling hot water
4 tbsp olive oil
2 large onions, peeled and very finely chopped
4 carrots, peeled and very finely chopped
2–3 celery sticks, very finely chopped
1 tsp sea salt flakes
6 large garlic cloves, finely grated or chopped
2 lbs 4 oz (1 kg) ground beef
3 tbsp *tatlı biber salçası* (Turkish sweet/mild red pepper paste)
10½ oz (300 g) chestnut/ cremini mushrooms, very finely chopped
¾ tsp coarse black pepper
2 tsp dried oregano
Scant 1 cup (200 ml) red wine
1 tbsp pomegranate molasses
1 tbsp balsamic vinegar
1 x 1 lb 9 oz (690 g) jar passata
1 x 14 oz (400 g) can finely chopped tomatoes
Scant ½ cup (100 ml) milk
2 bay leaves
A few sprigs of fresh thyme
1 cinnamon stick

In a jug, whisk the crumbled stock cube into the boiling water until fully dissolved, and leave to one side.

Add the olive oil to a large pot and place over low-medium heat.

Once hot, add the finely chopped onions, carrots and celery to the pot, sprinkle in half of the sea salt and soften and caramelize the vegetables for 15–20 minutes, stirring occasionally.

Add the garlic and beef to the pot, turn up the heat and, using the back of a wooden spoon, break up the meat in the pot. After 5–6 minutes, and once the meat has browned, add the *tatlı biber salçası* and mix it fully into the meat. Add the mushrooms, keeping the heat up high, then stir and season with the remaining salt, the black pepper and oregano.

Add the red wine and let it bubble vigorously for a few minutes until it reduces fully into the mince.

Stir in the pomegranate molasses and balsamic vinegar, then pour in the passata and chopped tomatoes. Stir again and fill the passata bottle up with a scant 1 cup (200 ml) of cold water, swish the water around, then pour the water from the bottle into the jug of stock to bring the liquid up to 2½ cups (600 ml).

Pour the stock and milk into the pot, stir, add the bay leaves, sprigs of thyme and the cinnamon stick and bring everything up to a boil. Turn the heat down and simmer on low-medium heat, with the lid half on, for 1–1½ hours, or until it reduces and the sauce thickens. Alternatively, add another scant 1 cup (200 ml) of water to the stock, turn the heat right down and cook for a minimum of 3 hours, covered, for a richer, slow-cooked ragù. Remove the bay leaves and cinnamon stick before serving.

When my children see this dish coming out of the oven, their smiles literally reach their ears. In Turkish, it's called Fırında Sebzeli Köfte Dizmesi which literally translates as "aligned oven-baked vegetables and patties."

Juicy Baked *Köfte* & Vegetables

ALL IN ONE

SERVES 4–6
Prep: 30 minutes
Cook: 1½ hours

—

2 medium eggplants, sliced into ¾ in (2 cm) rounds
1¼ tsp fine sea salt
Scant ½ cup (100 ml) milk
Scant 1 cup (100 g) fresh white breadcrumbs
1 lb 2 oz (500 g) beef or ground lamb
1¾ oz (50 g) fresh flat leaf parsley leaves, very finely chopped
2 tsp dried mint
4 garlic cloves, finely grated
¾ tsp coarse black pepper
1 egg
3 tbsp olive oil
14 oz (400 g) Cyprus or Russet potatoes, peeled and cut into ¾ in (2 cm) thick discs
2 large beefsteak tomatoes, sliced into ¾ in (2 cm) rounds
1 large onion, peeled and cut into ¾ in (2 cm) rounds
1 chicken stock cube, crumbled
2 tbsp *tatlı biber salçası* (Turkish sweet/mild red pepper paste)
2 cups (500 ml) boiling hot water

Preheat the oven to 425°F (220°C).

Place the sliced eggplants in a colander over a large bowl, sprinkle in ¼ teaspoon of the salt, give them a gentle toss, and leave for 15 minutes to release any excess moisture.

Pour the milk into a large bowl and mix in the breadcrumbs. Let it sit for a couple of minutes before adding the ground meat, parsley, dried mint, garlic, ¾ teaspoon of sea salt and most of the black pepper. Crack in the egg and bind the mixture together with clean hands.

Wet your hands with cold water and form the mixture into 12 equal-sized patties (around 2¼ oz/65 g each).

Wash your hands and pat dry the eggplant slices with paper towels, then brush the inside of a large Dutch oven, lidded casserole dish or roasting pan (either circular, around 11–12 in/ 28–30 cm in diameter, or rectangular around 10 x 12 in/25 x 30 cm) with 1 tablespoon of the olive oil. Stack the vegetables and patties on their sides, upright in the greased pan in some kind of consecutive fashion (potato, eggplant, patty, tomato, onion, etc). Brush the tops of the vegetables and patties with another tablespoon of olive oil and season the vegetables with the remaining salt. Place the pan on the middle rack of the oven and cook, uncovered, for 20 minutes.

Meanwhile, prepare the stock. In a jug, whisk the crumbled stock cube and *tatlı biber salçası* into the boiling water until dissolved.

Take the pan out of the oven, carefully pour in the stock, drizzle on the remaining olive oil and season the vegetables with the remaining black pepper. Pop the lid on (or, using a pair of oven gloves, very carefully cover tightly with foil), and bake for 45–50 minutes. Remove from the oven, carefully remove the lid or foil, then spoon the juices over the patties and vegetables, and put back in the oven, uncovered, for a final 5–10 minutes. Remove the pan from the oven and, if possible, let it sit, with the lid on, for 30 minutes before serving. Perfect with the Caramelized Onion & Orzo Basmati Rice (page 121) or plain yogurt and crusty bread.

I remember my mom regularly preparing this meal on a Tuesday afternoon, ready for me, my sister and brother to eat in the early evening. She would then reheat it for her and my dad once he'd got home from soccer training and we were in bed, along with half a loaf of stale bread that she would bring back to life by splashing it with water followed by a brief stint in the residual heat of the oven for a few minutes. Over the years, it has become a trusty Sunday afternoon meal for my family, as I can throw it in the oven and pretty much forget about it, and using cheaper cuts such as lamb neck chops on the bone makes it much more affordable.

Fırın Kebabı ONE-PAN LAMB & POTATO ROAST
QUICK PREP, SLOW COOK

SERVES 4-6
Prep: 20 minutes
Cook: 2 hours
—
1 chicken stock cube, crumbled
2 tbsp tomato paste
2 tbsp *tatlı biber salçası* (Turkish sweet/mild red pepper paste)
1¼ cups (300 ml) boiling hot water
Scant 1 cup (200 ml) cold water
8 large lamb neck chops on the bone (approx. 7 oz/200 g each)
2 large yellow onions, peeled, halved and thickly sliced
6 large Cyprus, Russet or Yukon Gold potatoes, peeled and halved
6 large garlic cloves, peeled and bashed
4 tbsp extra virgin olive oil
1 tsp sea salt flakes
¾ tsp coarse black pepper
1 oz (25 g) fresh flat leaf parsley, finely chopped
1 x 14 oz (400 g) can chopped tomatoes
2 bay leaves

Preheat the oven to 375°F (190°C).

In a jug, whisk the crumbled stock cube, the tomato paste and *tatlı biber salçası* into the boiling water until fully dissolved. Whisk in the cold water, and leave to one side.

Place the lamb, onions, potatoes and garlic cloves in a large, deep roasting pan and drizzle over half of the extra virgin olive oil. Mix everything together well with clean hands, then add the salt, black pepper and parsley and mix again. Evenly pour over the chopped tomatoes, using a large spoon to spread them over and into the rest of the ingredients. Add the bay leaves to the pan, pour over the stock, and seal the pan very tightly with foil.

Place the pan on the middle rack of the oven and cook for 1½ hours. After this time, remove the pan from the oven and carefully take off the foil. Drizzle 1 tablespoon of the extra virgin olive oil over the steaming lamb and potatoes, turn the heat up to 425°F (220°C) and cook for a further 25–30 minutes, uncovered, turning the chops over halfway through and drizzling over the remaining olive oil. Both the lamb and potatoes should be deliciously soft and tender, and charred at the edges when ready.

Take the pan out of the oven, cover with the foil again, and let it rest for 10 minutes. Remove the bay leaves before serving.

This is a dish of pure, layered, oozy Meliz Cooks-style comfort. I use half a frozen batch of the Slow-Cooked Bolonez (page 153) in this recipe, but if you'd like to make the bolonez *from scratch then give yourself enough time to do so before starting the béchamel sauce. The lasagne can be assembled the day before and stored in the fridge, or assembled then frozen, before it's baked. If freezing, wrap tightly in plastic wrap, freeze, then defrost in the fridge overnight, and bake in a preheated oven at 400°F (200°C)—bring up to room temperature or be prepared to give it at least 20 minutes over the suggested cooking time if it's fridge-cold when it goes into the oven, to ensure it's cooked through and piping hot throughout before serving.*

Hellimli Lasagne

TRADITIONAL FLAVORS, NEW RECIPE

SERVES 6–8
Prep: 25 minutes
Cook: 50 minutes
——

For the béchamel sauce:
5 tbsp (75 g) unsalted butter
⅔ cup (75 g) all-purpose flour
3¾ cups (900 ml) milk
A pinch of ground nutmeg
¼ tsp fine sea salt
A pinch of coarse black pepper
1 bay leaf
4½ oz (125 g) *hellim* (halloumi cheese), finely grated
1 tsp dried mint

For the basil & mint pesto:
3 tbsp toasted pine nuts
1 oz (30 g) fresh basil leaves
1 oz (30 g) fresh mint leaves
1 oz (25 g) *hellim* (halloumi cheese), finely grated
1 small garlic clove, peeled
Scant ½ cup (100 ml) extra virgin olive oil + extra for greasing

For the lasagne:
½ batch of the Slow-Cooked *Bolonez* (page 153)—if frozen, defrost in the fridge overnight
1 oz (25 g) fresh basil leaves, finely chopped
7 oz (200 g) mozzarella cheese, grated
16–20 dried lasagne sheets
3½ oz (100 g) *hellim* (halloumi cheese), finely grated

To make the béchamel, add the butter to a large saucepan and place on the stovetop over medium heat. Once melted, add the flour and keep whisking until it forms a smooth roux (like a paste). Add a third of the milk, plus the nutmeg, fine sea salt, coarse black pepper and bay leaf, whisking constantly. Slowly pour in the remaining milk while still whisking until all of the milk has been added. Once the sauce has thickened and starts to bubble a little, take the pan off the heat, remove the bay leaf, stir in the grated *hellim* and dried mint, and leave to one side.

Preheat the oven to 425°F (220°C).

To make the pesto, blend together all the ingredients, except the olive oil, in a food processor. Slowly pour the oil in while the food processor is still running until you get to your desired consistency.

Heat up the *bolonez* in a large saucepan over medium heat, and once bubbling, stir through the finely chopped basil, then remove the pan from the heat (if you are not using pre-prepared *bolonez*, then give yourself a couple of hours to prepare and cook the *bolonez* before you start the béchamel).

Brush the bottom of a large baking dish with olive oil, then start layering up your lasagne; start with a layer of the *bolonez*, followed by the béchamel, a little of the mozzarella, then some lasagne sheets, more *bolonez*, then béchamel, then lasagne sheets. Keep going until all of the elements have been used up, saving extra béchamel for the top and drizzling the pesto only on top of the lasagne and the layer beneath it. Finish off with the remaining mozzarella and finely grated *hellim*, then place on the middle rack of the oven and bake for 45–50 minutes, until deliciously golden brown. Leave to rest for 20 minutes before serving.

I met my very special friend Elyse when we were in high school together; our love of the performing arts solidified our friendship, as did our love of food. Elyse would be over at my house for köfte *and* dolma *on a Thursday night, and I'd be over at her house for salt beef and fries on a Friday, with her mom, dad and nana. Ironically, Elyse is now a vegan. The cooked, cooled salt beef stores well in the fridge, covered tightly with plastic wrap for 3 days. You can even freeze the cooked slices of salt beef (wrapped in parchment paper and then tightly with plastic wrap) for up to a month (defrost in the fridge before eating).*

Salt Beef & Zingy Coleslaw

QUICK PREP, SLOW COOK

SERVES 6–8
(WITH LEFTOVERS FOR
SANDWICHES THE NEXT DAY)
Prep: 20 minutes
Cook: 4 hours 10 minutes
——

For the salt beef:
3 lb 5 oz (1.5 kg) salt beef brisket
2 large carrots, peeled
   and left whole
2 large celery sticks + leaves, halved
2 large raw beets, peeled
4 garlic cloves, peeled and left whole
1 tbsp black peppercorns
1 red onion, peeled and halved
2 bay leaves
A few sprigs of fresh thyme

For the coleslaw:
9 oz (250 g) white cabbage,
   very finely shredded
5½ oz (150 g) red cabbage,
   very finely shredded
2 large scallions, very
   finely sliced on the diagonal
2 large carrots, peeled and coarsely
   grated/cut julienne-style
1 oz (25 g) fresh flat leaf parsley
   leaves, finely chopped
2 tbsp white wine vinegar
1 tbsp wholegrain mustard
1 tsp sea salt flakes
½ tsp coarse black pepper
1 tsp celery salt
1 tsp runny honey
Zest of 1 unwaxed lemon,
   finely grated
1⅓ cups (300 g) mayonnaise

Place the salt beef brisket in a large soup pot and cover with cold water. Add the rest of the salt beef ingredients to the pan and place on the stovetop over medium heat. Once the water comes up to a boil, turn the heat down to a low simmer and cook for 4 hours, half-covered, and ensure to skim off and discard any foam that rises to the surface of the simmering water as the salt beef cooks.

To make the coleslaw, add all the ingredients to a large bowl just before you are ready to serve, and mix together well so that all the shredded vegetables are coated liberally in the dressing.

Once the beef is cooked, remove from the pot, rest for 5 minutes and then thinly carve to serve alongside the coleslaw and some crunchy potatoes, or in a sandwich with English mustard and pickled cucumbers and pearl onions.

NOTE
If you'd prefer to prepare the coleslaw in advance, then mix together the shredded cabbages, scallions, carrots and parsley, place in a colander over a bowl, cover with plastic wrap and refrigerate until ready to use. Mix together the remaining mayonnaise dressing ingredients in a small bowl or plastic container and refrigerate until ready to use. Before dressing the coleslaw, ensure to fully drain any excess liquid from the vegetables. Transfer the shredded vegetables to a large serving dish, then stir in the mayonnaise dressing and serve.

Beautiful, creamy mash is given a little uplift in this recipe with a crunchy, seeded topping, rather like that of a cottage or shepherd's pie. It's seasoned with Parmesan or Grana Padano cheese and soft buttery cloves of garlic, and can be prepared a day in advance (keep in fridge overnight) and then brought up to room temperature and baked. Alternatively you could bake it, cool it, freeze it, then simply defrost, and reheat in a preheated oven at 400°F (200°C), covered with foil for the first 10 minutes and then uncovered for another 15–20 minutes until piping hot.

Baked Garlicky Parmesan & Sesame Mash

QUICK PREP, SLOW COOK

SERVES 6–8
Prep: 10 minutes
Cook: 1 hour

—

2 lb 4 oz (1 kg) Russet potatoes,
   peeled and cut into 2 in
   (5 cm) pieces
6 large garlic cloves,
   peeled and left whole
Generous 1 cup (275 ml) milk
3½ tbsp unsalted butter
1 bay leaf
4½ oz (125 g) Parmesan
   or Grana Padano cheese,
   finely grated
¾ tsp sea salt flakes
¼ tsp coarse black pepper
1 tsp sesame seeds
½ tsp fresh thyme leaves

Preheat the oven to 400°F (200°C).

Add the potatoes and whole garlic cloves to a large pot, cover with cold water and place on the stovetop over high heat. Bring up to a boil, then simmer for 15–20 minutes, until tender. Drain them fully of any water in a colander, allowing them to steam dry for a couple of minutes. Mash the potatoes and garlic, twice, through a ricer/sieve, then place the garlicky mashed potatoes back in the dry pan and put the lid on to keep them warm.

Either add the milk, butter and bay leaf to a heatproof jug and heat up in the microwave (on high) for a minute or two until piping hot, or add the milk, butter and bay leaf to a saucepan and place on the stovetop over medium-high heat until piping hot. Carefully remove the bay leaf.

The potatoes should still be a little hot once mashed, so carefully pour the hot buttery milk into the pot, along with 2 oz (60 g) of the grated cheese, the salt and black pepper and stir until melted. Place the cheesy mashed potatoes into a small, deep ovenproof dish and give it a few swirls with the back of a large spoon. Top with the remaining cheese, the sesame seeds and thyme leaves, and bake in the oven for 20–25 minutes or until crispy and caramelized on top and piping hot. Serve immediately.

I remember vividly watching my mom make her mashed potato-topped pies for us. My mom only ever uses her grandmother's dough and meat filling recipes when making traditional börek, *and she'd use them to make these Sunday afternoon pies too. I have also provided you with a gluten-free recipe for the dough—gluten-free dough is a little trickier to work with, so be patient, and be prepared to patch up a few little bits here and there, it won't be the end of the world. These pies can be baked, frozen, then defrosted at room temperature and baked in a preheated oven at 375°F (190°C) for 15–20 minutes or until piping hot.*

Mash-Topped Meat *Börek*

TRADITIONAL FLAVORS, NEW RECIPE

MAKES 8
PREP: 1 hour
COOK: 30 minutes

—

For the *pide* dough:
1 cup (250 ml) lukewarm water
1 tsp fine sea salt
1 tsp sugar
4 cups (500 g) all-purpose flour
+ extra for dusting
1 tsp baking powder
¼ cup (50 g) plain yogurt
3 tbsp + 1 tsp extra virgin
olive oil
1 medium egg, beaten

For gluten-free *pide* dough:
⅔ cup (150 ml) lukewarm water
1 tsp fine sea salt
1 tsp sugar
4 cups (500 g) gluten-free
self-rising flour
+ extra for dusting
1 tsp baking powder
½ tsp xanthan gum
⅔ cup (150 g) plain yogurt
2 tbsp + 1 tsp extra virgin
olive oil
1 medium egg, beaten

For the topping:
1 batch of Baked Garlicky
Parmesan & Sesame Mash
(unbaked, see page 162)
Olive oil, to drizzle

Continued overleaf

Add the lukewarm water to a small measuring jug and stir in the salt and sugar until fully dissolved. Add the flour and baking powder (and the xanthan gum if making the gluten-free pastry) to a mixing bowl, stir well, make a well in the center, then add the yogurt, 3 tablespoons of the extra virgin olive oil (or 2 tablespoons if making gluten free) and the lukewarm water mixture to the bowl. Using a fork, start to mix the wet ingredients into the dry ingredients and then bring the dough together with your hands. Once the dough starts to come together, turn it onto a clean surface and form into a smooth ball. Grease the dough and bowl with 1 teaspoon of the extra virgin olive oil, put the dough back in the bowl, then cover with a clean tea towel and leave to rest somewhere warm and cozy for 30 minutes.

Start to prepare your mash as per the recipe on page 162, firstly by boiling the potatoes and garlic while you cook the filling.

To make the meat filling (ingredients list overleaf), add the olive oil to a large frying pan and place on the stovetop over low-medium heat. Once the oil is hot, add the onion, followed by the sea salt flakes, and cook for 5–6 minutes, stirring occasionally, before adding the parsley stalks. Cook for another 2–3 minutes until softened and caramelized.

Add the ground beef to the pan, and using the back of a wooden spoon or spatula, break it down into the onion, so there are no big chunks of meat clumped together. Turn up the heat and brown for 3–4 minutes without stirring until the underside crisps up. Turn the heat back down, add the mushrooms, cook for a further 3–4 minutes, then add the dried mint and some salt and black pepper to the pan, stir well, then cook for a couple of minutes

Recipe continued overleaf

For the meat filling:
2 tbsp olive oil
1 large yellow onion,
    peeled and very finely chopped
¾ tsp sea salt flakes, + extra
    to taste
1 oz (30 g) fresh flat leaf parsley,
    leaves and stalks finely
    chopped but kept separate
    from each other
1 lb 2 oz (500 g) ground beef
5½ oz (150 g) white/
    chestnut/cremini
    mushrooms,
    very finely chopped
2 tsp dried mint
1 tsp coarse black pepper

more. Take the pan off the heat and stir in the finely chopped parsley leaves. Allow the filling to cool down a little before assembling the *börek*, and use this time to finish making the mashed potatoes (without topping them with the remaining Parmesan or Grana Padano, sesame seeds and thyme or baking—this will be done later).

Meanwhile, preheat the oven to 400°F (200°C). Line two large, shallow baking pans with parchment paper and brush the paper with the remaining 1 tbsp extra virgin olive oil.

Weigh the dough and divide into 8 equal portions. Roll each portion into a smooth ball, then dust a large clean surface with some flour (if making the gluten-free dough, dust a small piece of parchment paper with flour to roll the dough on, as it will be easier to lift and slide the flat disc of pastry onto the greased parchment paper lining the pan this way).

Place one of the balls onto the floured surface, dust the rolling pin and the top of the dough ball with flour, and start rolling out the pastry, turning the pastry 45 degrees each time you roll to create an even circular shape, around 6 in (15 cm) in diameter. Place the pastry disc onto a lined baking pan and repeat with the seven remaining pieces of dough, placing four discs on each baking pan. Using a fork, prick the center of each pastry disc a few times.

Fill the center of each pastry disc with an equal portion of the meat filling and pinch together the edges of each disc to create four corners, lifting the sides of the pastry slightly over the filling. Top the center of each pie with a generous portion of the mashed potatoes so that the filling isn't really visible. Brush the exposed dough with the beaten egg, which will give the cooked pastry a lovely golden color. Using a fork, create little flicks in the mashed potatoes, then top with the remaining grated cheese, sesame seeds and thyme leaves, and drizzle with a little olive oil.

Bake in the oven for 25–30 minutes or until golden brown all over with a crispy base. Serve with steamed greens (and a drizzle of hot instant gravy, if you want the full retro experience).

Roasted potatoes are 100% my ultimate weakness (photo on page 169). I could have them every day of the week. I've put my top tips for perfect roasted potatoes on page 135.

Crunchy Herby Roasted Potatoes

QUICK PREP, SLOW COOK

SERVES 4–6
Prep: 20 minutes
Cook: 1½ hours

—

6 tbsp light olive oil
4 lbs 8 oz (2 kg) Russet
   or Yukon Gold potatoes,
   unpeeled
2 tbsp cornstarch
12 garlic cloves, left whole
   and unpeeled
1 tsp sea salt flakes
A few sprigs of fresh rosemary

TIP

Turn to page 135 for tips on cooking perfect roasted potatoes every time.

Preheat the oven to 425°F (220°C). Add the olive oil to a large, shallow roasting pan.

Peel and wash the potatoes, then halve and quarter them into 1½–2 in (4–5 cm) chunks. Place into a large pot, wash with cold water, drain, then fill up the pot with cold water so the potatoes are fully immersed. Place the pot on the stovetop over medium-high heat, bring up to a boil and simmer for 8 minutes. Once the potatoes are cooking, put the roasting pan on the middle rack of the oven for 20 minutes until the oil is smoking.

After 8 minutes, drain the potatoes in a colander, ensuring that there is no water left in the pot at all, then place the potatoes back in the dry pot, sprinkle over the cornstarch, put the lid on the pot and give it all a good shake. Check to see that the potatoes are fluffy and fully coated in the cornstarch, then put the lid back on for another 5 minutes. While you wait, gently bash the garlic cloves with a rolling pin just so they slightly crack but aren't fully crushed, and the skins open a little.

Carefully take the roasting pan out of the oven and place on a flat, heatproof surface. Using a large pair of tongs, carefully place the potatoes into the hot oil, and once they are all in, gently turn them over and carefully tilt the pan to coat the tops of the potatoes with the hot oil. Sprinkle the potatoes with the sea salt, put the pan back on the middle rack of the oven and turn the heat down to 400°F (200°C).

Roast the potatoes for an initial 35–40 minutes or until the undersides really crisp up, then take the pan out of the oven, turn over the potatoes, add the rosemary and the bashed garlic to the pan and roast for another 20 minutes before turning the potatoes again. Place the pan back in the oven for another 15–20 minutes or until the potatoes are crunchy and a rich golden-brown color all over.

Transfer the potatoes to a platter using a spatula, ensuring you drain as much hot oil from them as possible. These are delicious served with the Salt Beef (page 160) or the Delicious Beef Short Ribs (page 168), and are the perfect accompaniment to any roast dinner.

This is the kind of dish that needs a bit of care put into it for the first 5–10 minutes, and then it can just be left to do its juicy, slow-cooked delicious thing in the oven (or slow cooker, page 208) for a few hours. Serve this with the Baked Garlicky Parmesan & Sesame Mash (page 162) and some steamed green beans dressed with olive oil and sea salt.

Delicious Beef Short Ribs

QUICK PREP, SLOW COOK

SERVES 4-6
Prep: 15 minutes
Cook: 4½ hours
—

1 beef stock cube, crumbled
2 tbsp *tatlı biber salçası*
  (Turkish sweet/mild
  red pepper paste)
2 tbsp beef gravy granules
2 tbsp pomegranate molasses
1 tbsp Worcestershire sauce
3 cups (750 ml) boiling
  hot water
6 large (around 1 lb 2 oz/500 g
  or each) beef short ribs
1 tsp sea salt flakes
3 tbsp olive oil
1 tsp coarse black pepper
2 large onions, peeled and
  finely chopped
2 large carrots, peeled and
  roughly chopped
2 large celery sticks,
  roughly chopped
6 garlic cloves, peeled
  and left whole
A few sprigs of fresh rosemary
A few sprigs of fresh thyme
2 bay leaves

Preheat the oven to 375°F (190°C).

In a jug, whisk the crumbled stock cube, *tatlı biber salçası*, gravy granules, pomegranate molasses and Worcestershire sauce into the boiling water until fully dissolved.

Season the short ribs with the sea salt flakes. Add 1 tablespoon of the olive oil to a large, deep sauté pan and place over medium heat. Sear the well-seasoned short ribs, two at a time, in the hot oil until browned all over, then put them in a large, deep Dutch oven or lidded casserole dish and season with the coarse black pepper.

The short ribs can release a lot of fat while cooking, so if the oil in the pan looks like it needs replacing, carefully discard it, wait for the pan to cool down for a couple of minutes, then give it a quick wipe or wash, ready to re-use.

In the pan you used to sear the ribs, add the remaining 2 tablespoons of olive oil, and place over medium heat. Once hot, add the onions and soften for 4–5 minutes before adding the carrots, celery, garlic cloves, rosemary, thyme and bay leaves. Once the garlic and herbs are fragrant, pour in the stock mixture, let it come to a boil, then take the pan off the heat.

Pour the sauce over the ribs in the Dutch oven or casserole dish. Place the lid on (or cover tightly with foil if you don't have a lid), and cook on the bottom rack of the oven for 3½ hours (give the ribs a gentle stir/turn halfway through). After this time, take off the lid (or foil), flip the short ribs over, and cook (uncovered) for a further and final 30 minutes or until the meat is tender and falling off the bone.

Transfer the short ribs and vegetables to a plate and cover them tightly in foil, discarding the bay leaves and herb stalks. Strain the sauce from the pot or dish into a large jug. Tilt the jug, and using a large spoon, separate the fat from the top of the sauce and discard sensibly (do not pour the fat down the sink).

If the sauce needs thickening at this point, transfer it to a pan and place on the stovetop over high heat until it thickens and reduces by one-third. Spoon the gravy over the short ribs to serve.

SWEET TREATS
& EASY BAKES

I have to be totally upfront here: I'm not as well known for my desserts, and that's because I'd rather swirl a piece of fresh crusty bread into a creamy mezze dish than dig into something sweet. When I do make a dessert, I love the contrast of crisp and creamy textures, and crave the harmonious surprise when pairing sweetness with savory saltiness. So here you'll find light and crisp *yufka* filled with tahini *helva*, in my *Tahın Helvalı Sigara Böreği* (page 175), which are topped with vibrant green pistachios and floral rose petals. These tahini-stuffed *helva* rolls are best served hot, only take 10–15 minutes to put together and the same amount of time to cook. I suggest sourcing a pistachio *helva* for this recipe, if possible, for that extra crunch and nutty flavor you'll get when biting into these hot and crunchy morsels of utter deliciousness. These crispy, oozy rolls are elevated with a scoop of vanilla ice cream, or, if you can source some, *damla sakızlı dondurma* (mastic gum ice cream).

In the *Pilavuna* Muffins (page 176), salty *hellim* and sweet juicy raisins are baked together for a delicious combination. The *Pilavuna* Muffins freeze brilliantly and are excellent with a cup of tea; you could even dip them into honey if you fancy that extra little sugar hit. The sweet and salty culinary partnership evident in the muffins is not something unique to Cypriot recipes, but it certainly runs through many of the baked goods and pastry synonymous with the island's cuisine. As a result, these are also an excellent breakfast and snack option.

I love the thick, creamy yogurt frosting that balances beautifully against the sweet orange-blossom-water syrup in the Orange Drizzle Loaf Cake with Orange Blossom Yogurt Frosting (page 179).

I also enjoy taking the favorite desserts of my childhood in England and giving them a Cypriot twist, as my mother did for me, such as the Spiced Fruit *Baklava* Crumble (page 185) and the Crunchy Creamy Cherry "Mess" (page 182). Familiar comfort, full of surprisingly pleasing flavors.

The Crunchy Creamy Cherry "Mess" is a dessert that can be assembled quickly, as long as the yogurt is strained overnight to give it its thick and creamy, labneh-like consistency. You could even infuse the cherries in the syrup the day before and simply reheat them on the stovetop or in the microwave just before serving. Crumble the meringues into the dollops of strained yogurt, alternating with the warm, spiced cherries, and finish it all off with a drizzle of cinnamon honey and a dusting of crunchy nuts. I mean, that's an absolute crowd-pleaser right there.

Some of the desserts can be prepared in advance, such as the Caramelized Apple Yogurt Cake (page 180), and some of them are so easy that they can be prepped and cooked in the company of your guests.

I've included some savory bakes here too, including two breads and my foolproof Yorkshire pudding (popover) recipe. These make wonderful accompaniments to some of the meals in this book, and more. I rarely make Yorkshire Puddings (page 193) in real time, as making them in advance and freezing them is so much more efficient when I am short on time or oven space, especially when cooking an all-consuming roast dinner. I keep batches of Yorkshire puddings in the freezer, and simply reheat them in the oven, from frozen (see instructions on page 194), until piping hot all the way through and crispy on the outside.

They honestly taste as if you've just made them and crisp up so beautifully in the oven.

Don't cut any corners in the recipe; ensure to follow all the instructions in full for a batch of really impressive yorkies:

⊙ Follow the quantities exactly, weighing the flour, using medium eggs and measuring out the milk. Do not guess or eyeball the quantities. Season with a generous ½ teaspoon of fine sea salt.

⊙ Resting the batter in the fridge for the recommended time is crucial.

⊙ The Yorkshire Puddings should be the only things in the oven while they are cooking, so that they get the full attention from the cooking temperature, and to guarantee that the oven will be free of steam for maximum crispness, too.

Tahini helva *is made by combining a sizzling hot, water-based sugar syrup with tahini, and continuously stirring until the mixture thickens and then eventually sets. It's delicious (and rather indulgent), usually eaten at breakfast, spread onto bread or, my mom's favorite way, in between a hot, buttery pita. Here, I use pistachio helva to fill thin rolls of filo pastry.*

Tahın Helvalı Sigara Böreği TAHINI HELVA STUFFED FILO ROLLS
FAST AND FILLING

MAKES 8
Prep: 10–15 minutes
Cook: 5–10 minutes
——

12 oz (350 g) pistachio
   tahini *helva*
8 triangular-shaped sheets
   of filo pastry or *üçgen yufka*
1 cup (250 ml) sunflower oil
2 tsp confectioners' sugar
2 tbsp honey (or agave syrup)
2 tbsp crushed pistachios
Fresh or dried rose petals
   (optional)

NOTE
If you can't find triangular üçgen
yufka *(small, thick, triangular-shaped filo pastry), then you can use regular filo sheets folded in half (to create a double layer), then cut into triangles. However, please note that these filo sheets are a lot thinner than* üçgen
yufka, *so the texture of the cooked cigars will differ.*

Cut the rectangular block of *helva* horizontally into eight long and thin, equal pieces.

Place one of the triangular sheets of pastry on a clean surface with the straight edge closest to you and the long point furthest away, and brush it all over with a little cold water, to help seal it once rolled. Place one of the pieces of *helva* along the straight edge of the pastry closest to you, leaving a ¾ in (2 cm) perimeter around the *helva* so that you can tuck and fold over the top and sides of the pastry as you tightly roll it away from you. Ensure the sides and edges of the pastry are completely sealed so that the *helva* inside is not exposed at all (otherwise, the *helva* could seep into the hot oil and burn while the *börek* cook). Repeat this process until you have eight cigar-shaped rolls.

Add the sunflower oil to a large, shallow frying pan and place it on the stovetop over medium heat. If you have a thermometer, heat the oil to around 350°F (180°C). If you don't have one, you can drop in a piece of pastry to check if it sizzles—the pastry should sizzle and take a little time to turn a light golden-brown color, since this is how the rolls should cook, so that the pastry is light and crispy and the filling melts and is oozy.

Gently lower four of the rolls into the hot oil and cook for 1–2 minutes on each side until golden brown and crispy. Using a large, slotted spoon, transfer the golden rolls to a plate lined with a double layer of paper towels.

Repeat with the remaining four rolls, then transfer to individual plates or a platter. Dust with the confectioners' sugar, drizzle with the honey and sprinkle over the crushed pistachios and rose petals (if using). Serve the rolls immediately, with ice cream, while they are still hot.

These muffins are an homage to pilavuna, *a traditional Cypriot pastry, which I shared in Meliz's Kitchen. I use a combination of* hellim *(halloumi cheese) and a hard cheese—traditionally* talar peyniri *(Turkish) or* kefalotyri *(Greek), but Pecorino Romano or an aged Gruyère work well as substitutes. The cheeses, along with the mint and raisins, are brought together into a simple cake batter, then topped with seeds, giving you that* pilavuna *fix without the extra effort.*

Pilavuna Muffins

TRADITIONAL RECIPE, CHEATER'S VERSION

**MAKES 12 MUFFINS
(OR 1 LOAF)
Prep: 25 minutes
Cook: 20 minutes**

——

2 tbsp + ⅔ cup (150 ml) olive oil
1 small onion, peeled and
finely chopped
2 large eggs
¾ cup (180 ml) milk
**2⅔ cups (300 g) self-rising flour
(or 2⅔ cups/300 g gluten-
free self-rising flour + ¼ tsp
xanthan gum** for gluten free)
1 tsp baking powder
⅛ tsp ground cinnamon
¾ tsp fine sea salt
1 tsp sugar
⅔ cup (100 g) raisins,
soaked in hot water for
10 minutes, then drained
**4½ oz (125 g) mature Cheddar/
Gruyère/Pecorino Romano
cheese,** finely grated
5½ oz (150 g) *hellim* **(halloumi
cheese),** cut into ½ in (1 cm)
cubes, **+ 1 oz (25 g),**
finely grated
1½ tbsp dried mint
1 tsp sesame seeds
1 tsp nigella seeds
¼ tsp aniseed

Preheat the oven to 375°F (190°C). Line a 12-hole muffin pan with paper liners.

Add 2 tablespoons of the olive oil to a frying pan and place on the stovetop over low-medium heat. Once hot, add the onions to the pan and soften for 10–12 minutes until jammy and caramelized.

In a large bowl, whisk together the eggs. Add the milk and the remaining ⅔ cup (150 ml) of olive oil, and whisk again. Sift in half of the flour (and the xanthan gum if making them gluten-free), the baking powder, cinnamon, salt and sugar, whisking until smooth. Sift and whisk in the remaining flour, fold through the softened onion, the raisins, most of the finely grated hard cheese (reserving a couple of tablespoons to top the muffins with), the cubes of *hellim* and the dried mint. Generously and evenly heap the batter into the 12 paper liners lining the muffin pan.

Top each muffin with the reserved grated cheese, the grated *hellim* and the mixed seeds. Bake for 18–22 minutes on the middle rack of the oven or until golden brown and cooked through. Transfer to a cooling rack and serve warm. Once cooled, store, covered with foil, for up to 3 days at room temperature.

NOTES

To freeze, place the baked and cooled muffins into plastic containers lined with parchment paper or lay flat in sealed freezer bags. To reheat from frozen, place on a baking pan and onto the middle rack of a preheated oven at 350°F (180°C) for 10–15 minutes or until fully heated through and piping hot (check that they're not still frozen in the middle).

You can also bake this batter in a 9½ x 5 in (900 g) loaf pan lined with parchment paper in a preheated oven at 375°F (190°C) for 35–40 minutes until golden brown and cooked through. Once baked, take it out of the pan, with the paper, and allow to cool on a cooling rack for at least an hour before slicing.

This cake is based on my revani recipe, a cake that is traditionally made with a combination of semolina and all-purpose flour, and soaked in a spiced syrup, once cooked. I've swapped semolina for ground almonds to make it gluten free, soaked it in a fragrant, sticky orange drizzle infused with cinnamon and orange blossom water, and topped it with a beautifully thick, strained yogurt frosting. Store the frosted cake in the fridge, covered with foil, for up to 3 days—it will still be deliciously moist.

Orange Drizzle Loaf Cake with Orange Blossom Yogurt Frosting

TRADITIONAL FLAVORS, NEW RECIPE

SERVES 8–10
Prep: 20 minutes
(at least 12 hours for the yogurt to strain overnight)
Cook: 40 minutes
—

For the frosting:
Scant 1 cup (200 g) thick plain yogurt
1¾ tbsp confectioners' sugar
1 tsp freshly squeezed orange juice
¼ tsp finely grated orange zest
½ tsp orange blossom water
2 tbsp crushed pistachios

For the cake:
3 large eggs
¾ cup (150 g) sugar (preferably superfine)
¾ cup (175 ml) olive oil
⅔ cup (150 g) thick plain yogurt
½ tsp finely grated orange zest
½ tsp vanilla extract, or seeds from ½ vanilla pod
1¼ cups (150 g) all-purpose flour (or 1¼ cups/150 g gluten-free all-purpose flour + ¼ tsp xanthan gum if making the gluten-free version)
1 tsp baking powder
Generous 1 cup (100 g) ground almonds

For the drizzle:
Scant ½ cup (100 ml) freshly squeezed orange juice
1 tsp orange blossom water
2 tbsp sugar
1 cinnamon stick

To prepare the frosting, place a sieve over a large bowl, line it with a thick sheet of paper towel or a clean cheesecloth, and spoon in the plain yogurt. Cover with another sheet of paper towel and place in the fridge overnight, or for at least 12 hours until it's thick and the consistency of light cream cheese.

Preheat the oven to 375°F (190°C). Line a 9½ x 5 in (900 g) loaf pan with parchment paper.

For the cake, in a large bowl, whisk together the eggs and sugar for 2–3 minutes until light and fluffy. Add the olive oil, yogurt, orange zest and vanilla and whisk for 3–4 minutes more.

Sift in the flour (and the xanthan gum if making the gluten-free cake) and the baking powder, then add in the ground almonds, and gently mix until completely smooth.

Pour the cake batter into the lined loaf pan and bake in the oven for 35–40 minutes on the bottom rack of the oven until nicely browned (a toothpick should come out clean).

While the cake bakes, make the drizzle. Add the orange juice, orange blossom water, sugar and cinnamon stick to a small saucepan and place over low-medium heat, stirring until the sugar dissolves. Once the liquid starts to bubble, take the pan off the heat, allow to cool, then discard the cinnamon stick.

Take the pan out of the oven and, using a toothpick, make little holes all over the cake. Evenly pour over the drizzle and leave to cool.

Once the cake has cooled, take it out of the pan and place onto a flat serving dish or cake stand. Take the strained yogurt out of the fridge and place it into a large bowl. Add the confectioners' sugar, orange juice, most of the orange zest and the orange blossom water to the bowl, whisk well, top the cake with the yogurt frosting, then sprinkle with the crushed pistachios and remaining orange zest.

Ever since I was a child, whatever house I've lived in, there has always been at least one apple tree in the garden, and we always use the apples to make cakes and crumbles with. As I mention in the Spiced Fruit Baklava Crumble recipe (page 185), I love the contrast of the tang of caramelized fruit and a sweet base, and this is another recipe that satisfies those cravings for me. This cake stays beautifully soft covered with foil or in a covered cake stand for up to 3 days, and like most cakes, can also be wrapped up tightly and frozen, either whole or sliced, for up to 2 months (defrost at room temperature before eating).

Caramelized Apple Yogurt Cake

QUICK PREP, SLOW COOK

SERVES 12
Prep: 20 minutes
Cook: 45 minutes
——

1 large crisp, tart apple, halved, cored and thinly sliced (approx. 5½ oz/150 g when sliced)
2 tsp freshly squeezed lemon juice
4 large eggs
Scant 1 cup (175 g) sugar (preferably superfine)
1 tsp vanilla extract/ seeds from ½ vanilla pod
⅔ cup (150 ml) olive oil
¾ cup (175 g) plain yogurt
2 cups (250 g) self-rising flour (or 2 cups/250 g gluten-free self-rising flour + ¼ tsp xanthan gum, if making it gluten free)
1 tsp baking powder
½ tsp ground cinnamon
2 tbsp demerara or brown sugar
1 tbsp confectioners' sugar

Preheat the oven to 375°F (190°C).

Line an 8 in (20 cm) round cake pan with parchment paper, and leave to one side.

Place the sliced apples into a bowl, pour over the lemon juice and stir well. This will prevent the apples from turning brown. Leave to one side.

In a large mixing bowl, whisk together the eggs, sugar and vanilla for 3–4 minutes until light, fluffy and bubbly. Slowly pour in the olive oil, whisking as you do, then add the yogurt and whisk well again. Sift half of the flour (and the xanthan gum if making the gluten-free cake) and the baking powder into the bowl and whisk gently, then add the remaining flour and whisk gently until the batter is soft and free of lumps.

Drain the lemon juice from the apples, then add the cinnamon and 1 tablespoon of the demerara or brown sugar to the apple slices and mix well.

Pour the batter into the lined cake pan, top with the apples, sprinkle over the remaining 1 tablespoon of demerara or brown sugar, and then bake on the bottom rack of the oven for 40–45 minutes until golden brown, or until a toothpick comes out clean when inserted into the center of the cake. Leave the cake to cool for 10–15 minutes in the cake pan, then using the parchment paper, carefully lift it out onto a cooling rack and allow to cool fully before dusting with the confectioners' sugar.

Two of my most-loved, non Turkish-Cypriot desserts as a child were cold vanilla ice cream topped with hot, syrupy cherries (usually out of a can), and Eton Mess. Both quick and satisfying, I've tried to capture the nostalgic sentiment and flavors of both in this delicious dessert. The texture of an orange blossom-infused cream—made with thick, strained yogurt (süzme yoğurt), *instead of whipped cream—is contrasted with light, crunchy meringues, soft, syrupy hot cherries, a drizzle of cinnamon honey and crunchy nuts in every mouthful. I use pre-made meringues for this one (I'm a cheater).*

Crunchy Creamy Cherry "Mess"
TRADITIONAL FLAVORS, NEW RECIPE

SERVES 6
Prep: 10 minutes
(+ a minimum of 12 hours for the yogurt to strain overnight)
Cook: 10 minutes
——

2¼ cups (500 g) thick
    plain yogurt
9 oz (250 g) pitted morello
    or sour cherries, fresh
    or frozen
4 tbsp confectioners' sugar
1 cinnamon stick
2 tsp orange blossom water
3 tbsp honey
¼ tsp ground cinnamon
½ tsp vanilla extract, or seeds
    from ½ vanilla pod
8–10 meringue cookies
½ cup (50 g) pistachios,
    roughly chopped

Place a sieve over a large bowl, line it with a thick sheet of paper towels or a clean cheesecloth and spoon in the thick plain yogurt. Cover with another sheet of paper towel and place in the fridge to strain overnight, for a minimum of 12 hours. It should be thick and the consistency of light cream cheese when it's ready.

Place the cherries, 3 tablespoon of the confectioners' sugar, the cinnamon stick and 1 teaspoon of the orange blossom water into a small saucepan, stir well, and place on the stovetop over low-medium heat. Bring up to a boil, turn down the heat and simmer for 5 minutes until the syrup thickens a little. Take the pan off the heat and allow to cool for a minute until warm. Remove and discard the cinnamon stick.

In a small bowl, mix together the honey and ground cinnamon. Set to one side.

Take the strained yogurt out of the fridge and transfer it to a dry bowl. Stir the remaining 1 tablespoon of confectioners' sugar, the remaining 1 teaspoon of orange blossom water and the vanilla through the strained yogurt.

Break up the meringue cookies into pieces. Roughly distribute the broken meringue, sweetened strained yogurt and most of the warm cherries among six small serving dishes, trying not to do it in too orderly a fashion. Finish by topping each serving with a spoonful of the remaining cherries, a generous sprinkling of the pistachios, and drizzling over a lovely swirl of the cinnamon honey.

Alternatively, arrange everything in a large serving dish and allow your guests to serve themselves.

This has become my "I'll bring dessert" dessert. I love how the tartness of baked fruits can cut through the sweetness of a cake, tart or crumble. However, I always feel a little hard done by with regular crumbles and crisps, as the fruit stews at the bottom rather than caramelizing resplendently, like the topping, say, of a tarte tatin. So, I've flipped this dessert over and infused it with the mesmerizing flavors, scents and textures of a nutty baklava. Although I've written the recipe for peaches and plums, you really can use any fruit you'd typically use in a crumble, crisp or tart, hence the more generic title; peaches, nectarines, plums, apples, pears, rhubarb and berries all work brilliantly. And yes, you've guessed it, I've given tips to make it gluten-free and plant-based too.

Spiced Fruit *Baklava* Crumble

TRADITIONAL FLAVORS, NEW RECIPE

SERVES 8
Prep: 15 minutes
Cook: 40–45 minutes
(+ 30 minutes cooling time)
—
For the pistachio crumble:
1⅔ cups (200 g) all-purpose flour or (or 1⅔ cups/200 g gluten-free all-purpose flour + ¼ tsp xanthan gum if making gluten-free version)
½ tsp baking powder (gluten-free if needed)
½ cup (50 g) jumbo rolled oats or gluten-free jumbo rolled oats
½ cup (60 g) pistachios
¼ tsp ground cinnamon
10 tbsp (150 g) cold unsalted butter (or plant-based equivalent), cut into ¾ in (2 cm) cubes
¼ cup (50 g) soft dark brown sugar

For the orange blossom syrup:
1¼ cups (300 ml) cold water
½ cup (100 g) sugar
2 tbsp runny honey (or agave syrup)
1 tsp orange blossom water
Juice of ½ large orange
½ cinnamon stick
3 cloves

Continued overleaf

Preheat the oven to 400°F (200°C).

Line a 9 in (23 cm) diameter round pie dish with parchment paper.

Add all of the pistachio crumble ingredients to a food processor and pulse slowly until the butter starts to form large crumbs, but hasn't been ground down to a powder. Pour the mixture into the lined pie dish and press it down using your hands so that the top is completely flat. Bake in the oven on the middle rack for 15 minutes.

While the crumble base is baking, add all of the orange blossom syrup ingredients to a small saucepan and place on the stovetop over medium-high heat. Once it starts to boil, leave it on a high simmer for around 10–15 minutes until the mixture has thickened and reduced by half, then turn off the heat.

While the crumble is baking in the oven and the syrup is reducing on the stove, mix together the fruit slices, ground cinnamon, orange zest and orange juice in a bowl.

After the crumble base has been baking for 15 minutes, take it out of the oven, and scrape the flattened top a little with a fork so that the topping starts to resemble crumbs. Put it back in the oven on the middle rack for another 5 minutes until the top starts to look a little crunchier. Carefully take the dish out again, arrange the fruit slices on top of the crumbs, and scrape out any of the juicy residue left in the bowl and onto the fruit. Using a spoon, evenly pour the syrup over the fruit and crumbs. Sprinkle over the demerara or brown sugar and put the dish back onto the middle

Recipe continued overleaf

Spiced Fruit *Baklava* Crumble *CONTINUED*

For the topping:
**14 oz (400 g) ripe peaches/
  plums,** or a combination
  of both, pitted and cut
  into ½ in (1 cm) thick slices
½ tsp ground cinnamon
Zest of 1 large orange,
  finely grated
Juice of ½ large orange
1 tsp demerara or brown sugar
3 tbsp pistachios, ground
  in the food processor
  + extra to finish

rack of the oven. Bake for another 20–25 minutes, or until the fruit has softened, but is still tender, and the tops have just slightly caramelized.

Take the dish out of the oven, sprinkle over the ground pistachios so that they stick to the hot syrupy fruit, and let the crumble cool for at least 30 minutes before you try to remove it from the dish. Once cooled but still a little warm, gently lift the crumble out of the pie dish using the paper, and onto a large flat plate, carefully easing the paper out from underneath as you do so. Serve with whipped cream, custard or ice cream and an extra sprinkling of ground pistachios.

NOTES

This crumble can be made the day before, covered with foil and stored at room temperature. Reheat in the oven on the middle rack at 350°F (180°C) for 8–10 minutes, or until heated through, before serving, if required.

Alternatively, once cooked, you can also freeze the crumble (whole or portioned and stored in an airtight container) for up to 3 months. Either defrost in the fridge overnight and then reheat at 350°F (180°C) for 20–25 minutes, or until piping hot, or reheat from frozen for 30–35 minutes, again, until fully heated through. It will need less time (10–15 minutes) if you're only reheating individual portions and not the whole crumble.

In The Turkish-Cypriot dialect, these flatbreads are known as bidda *or* bitta, *and in Turkey, they are called* bazlama, *but whatever they are referred to as, there is no disputing that they are things of absolute beauty. Although the dough is yeasted, I also add milk and yogurt for that extra fluffy factor. If you want to keep them vegan-friendly, then use plant-based milk and yogurt. Warm, light and pillowy, they are delicious simply brushed with a little butter, and whether they are topped with grilled* hellim *(halloumi cheese) and drizzled with honey, dipped into cream cheese and sour cherry jam, or filled with some of the fakeout treats in Chapter 4, they are as joyous to watch rise and bubble in the pan as they are to eat.*

Fluffy *Bidda/Bazlama* Flatbreads

TRADITIONAL RECIPE, CHEATER'S VERSION

MAKES 6 FLATBREADS
**Prep: 2 hours 30 minutes
(including proofing time)
Cook: 15 minutes**

—

½ cup (125 ml) lukewarm water
**Scant ½ cup (100 ml) lukewarm
    milk**
1 tsp sugar
**1 x ¼ oz (7 g) envelope active
    dry yeast**
**4 cups (500 g) strong white
    bread flour** + extra for dusting
1 tsp fine sea salt
½ cup (100 g) plain yogurt
2 tbsp olive oil + little extra
    for greasing and brushing
**A large pat of salted
    or unsalted butter or
    plant-based equivalent,**
    to serve (optional)

Pour the water and milk into a jug, stir in the sugar to dissolve, then add the yeast. Leave somewhere warm and cozy for 5–10 minutes until the yeast activates and bubbles form in the liquid.

Sift the flour into a large bowl, stir in the salt, throw in the yogurt, drizzle in the olive oil, then gently pour in the activated liquid yeast mixture and mix to form a dough. Knead the dough for 8–10 minutes, either on a clean, flour-dusted work surface with your hands, or in a stand mixer or using a hand mixer with a dough hook until nice and smooth. Tuck the sides of the dough under to form a smooth ball, then place in a large bowl (greased with a little olive oil). Cover the bowl with plastic wrap and a tea towel and leave somewhere warm and cozy to proof for 1–1½ hours until doubled in size—it should look light, with even a few bubbles appearing on the top, as this is what will give the cooked *bidda* its fluffy, pillowy texture.

Once the dough has substantially risen, take it out of the bowl and gently punch it down a little (this is called knocking back—taking out the air bubbles which will form again after the shorter second proof) and then divide the dough into six equal pieces, roughly 5 oz (140 g) each in weight. Drizzle and lightly rub each piece of dough with olive oil, tuck the sides under, and using a little pressure between the palm of your hand and a clean work surface, roll each piece into a smooth ball. Leave all the dough balls on the work surface, cover with plastic wrap and a clean, light tea towel and leave to proof for another 30 minutes or so until they have almost doubled in size again. If your work surface is cold, place each ball on a large, lightly oiled tray, cover with plastic wrap and a tea towel and take them somewhere warm and cozy to proof.

Recipe continued overleaf

Fluffy *Bidda/Bazlama* Flatbreads *CONTINUED*

Place a medium-sized, nonstick frying pan on the stovetop to heat up over low-medium heat and start to roll out the *bidda*. Do not add any flour at this stage as the olive oil will keep them smooth and prevent them from sticking to the surface as you roll, or to the pan as they cook.

Using a rolling pin, roll out each of the balls into a circular disc, roughly 6½ in (17 cm) in diameter. To get them circular and uniform in shape, turn the dough at a 45 degree angle each time you roll. (I roll out one and while it's cooking, I roll out another, but if you have the space, feel free to roll them all out before cooking—you'll just need to work quickly so they don't dry out.)

Once the pan is hot, place one rolled dough into the pan and cook for around 1–2 minutes until bubbles form on the top and the underside is just slightly golden, then flip it over and cook the other side for another 30–60 seconds until bubbly and golden brown. Keep the cooked *bidda* covered and wrapped in tea towels to ensure they stay soft, warm and fluffy while you cook the remaining ones.

Serve them brushed with butter (brush them while they're still hot so that the butter melts) or serve as flatbread vessels and fill them up with the grilled meats, *köfte*, mezze and salad recipes from Chapter 4. If you want to prepare them earlier in the day, wrap them up tightly in parchment paper and tea towels to keep them soft. Then remove the tea towels and wrap in foil and reheat in an oven preheated to 325°F (170°C) for 5–10 minutes until warmed through. They can also be frozen, then defrosted and reheated in the oven in the same way.

These loaves really are a joy to make—with or without the seeds. I usually bake a double batch and freeze a couple so I always have some on hand. When you're ready for them, take them out of the freezer, defrost for an hour or so, then reheat in a preheated oven at 375°F (190°C) for 15–20 minutes or until the crust crisps up again and the inside is piping hot. Alternatively, bake, slice and freeze the slices for toast.

Susamlı Somun Ekmeği SIMPLE SEEDED LOAVES
TRADITIONAL FLAVORS, NEW RECIPE

MAKES 2 LOAVES
Prep: 2 hours (including proofing time)
Cook: 22 minutes
(+ 30 minutes cooling time)

—

1 cup (225 ml) lukewarm water
Scant ½ cup (100 ml) lukewarm milk
1 tsp sugar
1 x ¼ oz (7 g) envelope active dry yeast
4 cups (500 g) strong white bread flour + extra for dusting
1½ tsp fine sea salt
1 tbsp olive oil + a little extra for greasing

To coat:
1 tbsp all-purpose flour
2 tbsp milk
6 tbsp sesame seeds

Pour the lukewarm water and milk into a jug, stir in the sugar to dissolve, then add the yeast. Cover and leave somewhere warm and cozy for 5–10 minutes until the yeast activates and bubbles form in the liquid.

Sift the strong white bread flour into a large bowl, stir in the salt, make a well in the center, pour in the olive oil and liquid yeast mixture and mix to form a dough. Knead the dough for 10 minutes, either on a clean, flour-dusted work surface with your hands, or in a stand mixer or using a hand mixer with a dough hook until nice and smooth. Tuck the sides of the dough under to form a smooth ball, then place in a large bowl (greased with a little olive oil). Cover the bowl with plastic wrap and a tea towel and leave somewhere warm and cozy to proof for an hour or until doubled in size.

In a small bowl, mix together the all-purpose flour and milk for the coating to form a smooth paste. Pour the sesame seeds onto a large tray. Line a large, shallow baking pan with parchment paper.

Once proofed, take the dough out of the bowl, knock it back by gently punching it down a couple of times, turn it over, stretch it out, tuck the sides under to form a large ball, then cut and divide the dough in half. Tuck the sides under each piece again, and roll each one into a smooth ball.

With the tucked-under side facing upwards, stretch out each ball into a disc with your hands until each one is around 6¼ in (16 cm) in diameter. Start to fold over the dough from the top of the disc (furthest away from you), downwards, pinching down into the dough laying flat on the surface, at around 1¼ in (3 cm) intervals, until you are left with a long baguette-shaped piece of dough around 9½ in (24 cm) in length. Ensure to pinch together the underside of the dough too.

Recipe continued overleaf

Repeat this process with the other piece of dough, then brush the tops and sides of each loaf with most of the flour and milk paste you made earlier. Put the baguettes, pasted-side down, onto the tray of sesame seeds, then brush the underside of the baguettes with the remaining paste, and turn over, ensuring to fully coat the loaves all over in the seeds. Once coated, place the loaves onto the lined baking pan, cover with plastic wrap or a light tea towel, and proof for another 30 minutes at room temperature.

Meanwhile, preheat the oven to 450°F (230°C).

Once proofed, take the covering off the baking pan, then cut a long deep slit along the top on one side of each of the baguettes. Place the pan in the oven, pour 3 tablespoons of cold water straight into the bottom of the oven to create steam and quickly close the oven door. Bake the loaves in the oven for 20–22 minutes or until they are golden brown and sound hollow when you tap the underside. Leave to cool on cooling racks for at least 30 minutes before cutting through so that the insides of the loaves turn lovely and fluffy.

I'll never forget the day when I walked into my mom and dad's kitchen to be greeted by a bowl of these on the counter. "Mom, what are these?!," I asked. "My hellimli *Yorkshire puddings," she responded. Yorkshire pudding is a type of popover usually served with roast beef as part of the traditional British Sunday roast. This adapted recipe has been a phenomenon since I first shared it, with people making them to serve with roast lamb or drizzled with honey and a cup of tea. I've given you my basic Yorkshire pudding recipe, including my gluten-free Yorkshire pudding recipe, as well as the infamous* hellimli *(with halloumi) version.*

Hellimli Yorkshire Puddings

TRADITIONAL RECIPE, CHEATER'S VERSION

MAKES 12
Prep: 5 minutes (+ at least 1 hour chilling time in fridge)
Cook: 50 minutes
—

**For the regular
Yorkshire pudding mix:**
Scant 1 cup (200 ml) milk
(whole, 2% or dairy-free such as almond, soy or oat are fine)
4 medium eggs
**Scant 1 cup (100 g) all-purpose
flour**
½ tsp fine sea salt
**3 tbsp sunflower/vegetable/
rice bran oil**

**For the gluten-free
Yorkshire pudding mix:**
Scant 1 cup (200 ml) milk
(whole, 2% or dairy-free such as almond, soy or oat are fine)
4 large eggs
**1¾ oz (50 g) gluten-free
all-purpose flour**
1⅓ cups (150 g) cornstarch
½ tsp fine sea salt
**3 tbsp sunflower/vegetable/
rice bran oil**

**For the *hellimli* topping
(optional):**
**3½ oz (100 g) *hellim*
(halloumi cheese),**
coarsely grated
1 tbsp dried mint
1 tsp sesame seeds
1 tsp nigella seeds

In a large measuring jug, whisk together the milk, eggs and all-purpose flour (plus the cornstarch if you are making the gluten-free version). Whisk until completely smooth and no lumps are visible, stir through the salt, then cover the jug and put it in the fridge for at least an hour or overnight.

Preheat the oven to 480°F (250°C).

When the oven is hot, fill each of the 12 holes of a deep, nonstick muffin pan with around ¾ teaspoon of the oil, ensuring you also grease the sides, to easily pop out the puddings once they're done.

Place the muffin pan on the top rack of the oven for 15–20 minutes until the oil is smoking.

If you are making the *hellimli* Yorkshire puddings, then mix together the topping ingredients while the muffin pan is in the oven. If you are making plain ones, leave out this step.

Take the Yorkshire pudding batter out of the fridge and give it a quick but thorough stir, as the flour has a tendency to settle at the bottom of the jug while it rests in the fridge (especially with the gluten-free batter).

Carefully take the muffin pan out of the oven and place it on an even, heatproof surface. In one swift motion, quickly pour equal measures of the batter around ¾ of the way up into the center of the sizzling hot oil in each of the 12 holes of the muffin pan without topping them up. If making the *hellimli* Yorkshire puddings, add a heaped teaspoon of the *hellimli* mixture to the center of the batter in each hole, then quickly and carefully place the muffin pan back on the middle rack of the oven, and

Recipe continued overleaf

immediately close the oven door. Turn the oven down to 410°F (210°C) and bake for 25–30 minutes. Do not open the oven door at all until the Yorkshire puddings are cooked and do not be tempted to take them out too early, otherwise they'll just collapse.

Once cooked, they should all be a rich, dark golden-brown color, look deliciously crispy and have fully risen. Take the Yorkshire puddings straight out of the muffin pan and onto a cooling rack, and either serve immediately, or allow to cool completely, put them in freezer bags and freeze for up to 6 months.

NOTE
To reheat (from frozen, as there is no need to defrost), place in a preheated oven at 410°F (210°C) for 8–10 minutes, and they'll taste as if you've just made them.

COOKING WITH AN AIR FRYER OR A SLOW COOKER

I am a traditionalist when it comes to cooking, and rely mostly on my stovetop, oven and the *mangal* (BBQ). I love the intensity and depth of flavor achieved by slowly cooking down a sauce or soup in a pot over low heat, caramelizing meat, pastries and vegetables in the oven, and grilling over hot coals. However, I fully value the appeal and popularity of portable appliances such as air fryers and slow cookers.

Air fryers are an excellent option for smaller households, and slow cookers give us the opportunity to let something delicious and nutritious bubble away throughout the day, in a low-energy appliance. The dishes I've recommended to cook in the slow cooker are the ones that I, myself, am happy to leave cooking away in one, but not without a few suggested tips.

In terms of using the slow cooker, I'd always suggest browning and softening vegetables or searing meat in a pan on the stovetop first (as you would using the traditional method), as this is when you can really pack in the flavor that is achieved through caramelization, sweetness and charred edges. You will not get the same outcome if you just throw everything into the slow cooker.

The recipes I've shared for the slow cooker, such as *Kıymalı Bezelye* (page 206) and Slow-Cooked *Bolonez* (page 207) are fine examples of this, and I would also suggest adding a scant 1 cup (200 ml) less liquid (stock) than the original recipes when using the slow cooker, while still ensuring that joints of meat are fully immersed in liquid while cooking. I have adjusted the liquid amounts for the suggested slow cooker methods accordingly; if you choose to experiment with any of the recipes in the book that are not on these pages, then please do reduce the amount of liquid in the same way.

Although I am told you can cook pretty much anything in an air fryer, I reserve cooking with them for when I want to cook quickly and cost-effectively, and to achieve a grilled and crispy finish to meat, fish and vegetables. The air fryer provides excellent, charred and juicy results when used to cook the spiced, coated fish fillets in the Tangy Fish Tacos (page 202) and the *Köfte* Kebabs (page 203).

If your air fryer has a double-basket, then you can cook two batches at once; if not, depending on the size of your air fryer baskets, you may have to halve the recipe or cook some of the recipes in two batches (such as the Spiced Roasted Cauliflower, Potatoes & Chickpeas on page 201, White Cheese & Spinach Open-Faced *Börek* on page 26, and Crispy Chicken Wings on page 106) to guarantee the best results. Obviously this would take a little longer, so you would need to keep the first batch warm while you cook.

Balık Ekmek-Style Smoked Mackerel Baguettes

TRADITIONAL RECIPE, CHEATER'S VERSION

SERVES 4
Prep: 10 minutes
Cook: 15 minutes
—

¼ cup (60 g) mayonnaise
½ tsp dried mint
1 large unwaxed lemon, finely zested and cut into 4 wedges
½ tsp coarse black pepper
4 small, fresh sandwich-size baguettes
4 large smoked mackerel fillets
1¾ oz (50 g) arugula leaves
1 large white onion, peeled and finely sliced
1 *kapya biber* (capia pepper), red romano or small red bell pepper, halved, deseeded and finely sliced
1 oz (30 g) fresh flat leaf parsley leaves, finely chopped
2 large, ripe tomatoes, thinly sliced
1 tsp sumac
2 tsp pomegranate molasses
½ tsp sea salt flakes
4 pickles, thinly sliced
1 tsp *pul biber* (Aleppo pepper/ Turkish red pepper flakes)

In a small bowl, mix together the mayonnaise, dried mint, lemon zest and coarse black pepper, and leave to one side.

Splash the baguettes with a little bit of cold water and place them in the air fryer. Bake at 350°F (180°C) for 4–5 minutes or until warm and crusty.

Heat the smoked mackerel fillets in the air fryer at 350°F (180°C) for 4–5 minutes or until piping hot.

While the baguettes and fish are in the air fryer, prepare the salad. Place the arugula leaves, onion, *kapya biber*, parsley, tomatoes and sumac in a large dish but do not stir until the baguettes and fish are ready.

Once the mackerel fillets are hot and crispy, use a knife and fork to carefully peel away the skin.

Drizzle the salad with the pomegranate molasses and sea salt and lightly toss together.

Slice the baguettes in half lengthways, and spread the prepared mayonnaise on the inside of each of the four top halves of the baguettes. Generously load the bottom half of each of the four baguettes with the salad, then top with the sliced pickles and finally the hot, smoked mackerel. Squeeze the juice from the lemon wedges over the mackerel, then sprinkle them with the *pul biber*. Place the tops of the baguettes on the sandwiches and devour your *balık ekmek*.

Loaded Hummus Topping No. 1:
Spiced Roasted Cauliflower, Potatoes & Chickpeas

ALL IN ONE

SERVES 4–6
Prep: 10 minutes
Cook: 25 minutes–1 hour
(depending on size
of air fryer)
—

1 x 14 oz (400 g) can chickpeas
   (8½ oz/240 g drained
   weight)
14 oz (400 g) baby potatoes,
   washed and halved
14 oz (400 g) cauliflower florets
2 tbsp cornstarch
3 tbsp olive oil
1 tsp sumac + extra to garnish
1 tsp ground cumin
   + extra to garnish
2 tsp paprika + extra to garnish
1 tsp *pul biber* (Aleppo pepper/
   Turkish red pepper flakes)
   + extra to garnish
2 tsp garlic powder
1 tsp sea salt flakes
½ tsp coarse black pepper
2 tsp dried oregano
1 tbsp sesame seeds
1 batch of Creamy Dreamy
   Hummus (page 63)
A small handful of fresh
   flat leaf parsley leaves,
   finely chopped
1 tbsp extra virgin olive oil

Drain the chickpeas fully through a sieve, place them on a large baking pan lined with a couple of sheets of paper towels, and gently pat and roll them dry with another couple of sheets of paper towels. Pat the potatoes and cauliflower dry with paper towels too—this will prevent the chickpeas and vegetables from releasing too much moisture while cooking and will also ensure that they crisp up beautifully.

Add the chickpeas, potatoes and cauliflower to a large bowl, sprinkle over the cornstarch and mix well with clean hands until fully coated—shaking the bowl a few times helps too.

Add 2 tablespoons of the olive oil to the bowl along with the sumac, cumin, paprika, *pul biber* and garlic powder and mix again, then add the remaining olive oil, salt, pepper, oregano and sesame seeds, and stir well again, shaking the bowl if necessary, to ensure everything is fully coated.

Line your air fryer with parchment paper and, depending on the size of the basket, cook the chickpeas, potatoes and cauliflower in two separate batches at 375°F (190°C) for 25–35 minutes (each batch) or until crunchy and cooked through, checking halfway through. If the potatoes need a little longer, then remove the chickpeas and cauliflower from the basket and keep the potatoes cooking for a few extra minutes until crispy and tender.

While the chickpeas and vegetables are in the air fryer, make the hummus (page 63), then spread it all over a large platter. Top with the roasted chickpeas and vegetables and an extra sprinkling of sumac, cumin, paprika and *pul biber* and the chopped parsley, and a generous drizzle of extra virgin olive oil. Serve with crusty bread.

Tangy Fish Tacos & Tahini Tartare

FAST AND FRESH

SERVES 4
Prep: 20 minutes
Cook: 6 minutes
—

For the red cabbage:
5½ oz (150 g) red cabbage,
  finely shredded
1 tbsp pomegranate molasses
1 tbsp freshly squeezed
  lime juice

For the tahini tartare:
⅓ cup (75 g) tahini
1½ tbsp ice-cold water
⅓ cup (75 ml) freshly squeezed
  lime juice
⅓ cup (75 g) mayonnaise
½ tsp coarse black pepper
1 tbsp finely chopped fresh
  cilantro leaves
1 tbsp capers, finely chopped
2 tbsp finely chopped pickles

For the fish:
4 large cod/haddock fillets
  (7 oz/200 g each),
  skinless and boneless
2 tsp sweet smoked paprika
2 tsp paprika
1 tsp *pul biber* (Aleppo pepper/
  Turkish red pepper flakes)
2 tbsp olive oil
1 tbsp pomegranate molasses
¼ tsp sea salt flakes
¼ tsp coarse black pepper

To serve:
8 corn tortillas
1 large ripe avocado,
  pitted, peeled and sliced
Fresh cilantro,
  roughly chopped
2 limes, cut into wedges
Pul biber (Aleppo pepper/
  Turkish red pepper flakes),
  to sprinkle

Add the finely shredded red cabbage to a bowl and mix together with the pomegranate molasses and lime juice. Set to one side.

Add the tahini, cold water and lime juice to a small bowl and whisk together until smooth (don't be alarmed; initially the dip will turn lumpy and look like it's curdled before it becomes smooth; be patient, ensure you use ice cold water, and you'll get there). Add the mayonnaise to the bowl, whisk into the tahini until smooth again, then add the remaining tartare ingredients and stir until fully combined.

Cut the fish fillets into large, chunky finger-sized pieces (approx. 1¼ x 3¼ in/3 x 8 cm) and pat each piece completely dry with paper towels. Mix the smoked paprika, paprika and *pul biber* together on a large tray or plate, then add the fish fillets to the ground spices and gently roll them around until they are fully coated. Drizzle over the olive oil and pomegranate molasses, sprinkle over the salt and black pepper, then roll the fish around again so that the fillets are covered in the sticky, oily spices. Line your air fryer with parchment paper and place the fish fillets inside. Cook the fish fillets in the air fryer at 410°F (210°C) for 5–6 minutes until cooked through and flaky.

When the fish fillets are almost cooked, put the tortillas into the microwave to warm up for the final minute or so, then serve them loaded with the tahini tartare sauce, pickled red cabbage, avocado, fish fillets and cilantro, with a generous squeeze of fresh lime juice and a sprinkling of *pul biber* on top.

Köfte Kebabs & Garlic Sauce
TRADITIONAL RECIPE, CHEATER'S VERSION

SERVES 4–6
Prep: 20 minutes (+ 1 hour
chilling time in fridge)
Cook: 15 minutes

—

For the *köfte*:
1 lb 2 oz (500 g) boneless, skinless
   chicken thighs, ground in a
   food processor, **or 1 lb 2 oz
   (500 g) ground lamb**
1 red onion, peeled and coarsely
   grated/finely chopped
   in a food processor
1 large *kapya biber* (capia
   pepper), red romano or
   small red bell pepper,
   halved, deseeded and finely
   chopped in a food processor
1 oz (30 g) fresh flat leaf
   parsley, leaves and stalks
   finely chopped
4 garlic cloves, finely grated
1 tsp *pul biber* (Aleppo pepper/
   Turkish red pepper flakes)
1 tsp paprika
1 tsp coarse black pepper
1 tsp sea salt flakes
1 tsp dried mint
2 tbsp *tatlı biber salçası*
   (Turkish sweet/mild
   red pepper paste)
3 tbsp extra virgin olive oil

For the garlic sauce:
1 tsp finely grated garlic
4 tbsp mayonnaise
½ cup (120 ml) runny plain
   yogurt
1 tsp extra virgin olive oil
½ tsp finely chopped fresh
   flat leaf parsley
1 tsp freshly squeezed
   lemon juice
¼ tsp dried mint
¼ tsp *pul biber* (Aleppo pepper/
   Turkish red pepper flakes)
½ tsp sea salt flakes
¼ tsp coarse black pepper

Add all the *köfte* ingredients, reserving 1 tablespoon of the extra virgin olive oil, to a large dish, mix everything together really well, then refrigerate the mixture for an hour.

Take the *köfte* mixture out of the fridge, wet your hands with cold water (so that the mixture doesn't stick to them) and shape into six long and even-sized *köfte*, each around 1½ x 7 in (4 x 18 cm) in length. Place them on a plate or tray lined with parchment paper to avoid sticking.

Using two fingers, gently push down to create indents all along the *köfte*, ensuring that the *köfte* keep their overall shape.

Line your air fryer with parchment paper. Brush the *köfte* with the remaining extra virgin olive oil, and depending on the size of your air fryer, you may or may not need to cook the *köfte* in two batches to ensure that they are all laying completely flat and not touching each other. Cook at 375°F (190°C) for around 15 minutes, until cooked through, turning over halfway through.

While the *köfte* are cooking, prepare your garlic sauce—mix together all the ingredients and refrigerate until ready to serve.

Once the *köfte* are cooked, take them out of the air fryer and serve immediately with the garlic sauce, some hot and fresh Fluffy *Bidda/Bazlama* Flatbreads (page 187) and any of the salads from this book.

Hellimli Yorkshire Puddings

TRADITIONAL FLAVORS, NEW RECIPE

MAKES 4
**Prep: 5 minutes (+ at least
1 hour chilling time in fridge)**
**Cook: 40 minutes–1 hour
20 minutes (depending on
size of air fryer)**

———

**For the regular Yorkshire
pudding mix:**
Scant 1 cup (200 ml) milk
  (whole, 2% or dairy-free such
  as almond, soy or oat are fine)
4 medium eggs
Scant 1 cup (100 g) all-purpose
  flour
½ tsp fine sea salt
3 tbsp sunflower/vegetable/
  rice bran oil

**For the gluten-free
Yorkshire pudding mix:**
Scant 1 cup (200 ml) milk
  (whole, 2% or dairy free such
  as almond, soy or oat are fine)
4 large eggs
Scant ½ cup (50 g) gluten-free
  all-purpose flour
1⅓ cups (150 g) cornstarch
½ tsp fine sea salt
3 tbsp sunflower/vegetable/
  rice bran oil

**For the *hellimli* topping
(optional):**
3½ oz (100 g) *hellim*
  (halloumi cheese),
  coarsely grated
1 tbsp dried mint
1 tsp sesame seeds
1 tsp nigella seeds

In a large measuring jug, whisk together the milk, eggs and flour (plus the cornstarch if you are making the gluten-free version). Whisk until completely smooth and no lumps are visible, stir in the salt, then put the jug in the fridge for at least an hour.

Fill four deep individual Yorkshire pudding pans with 1¼ tsp oil each.

Put the pudding pans in the air fryer and set the temperature to 425°F (220°C) for 14 minutes.

If you are making the topped Yorkshire puddings, then mix together the ingredients for the *hellimli* topping while the pans are heating up in the air fryer. If you are making plain ones, then you can leave out this step.

After the pans have been in the air fryer for 14 minutes, take the Yorkshire pudding batter out of the fridge and give it another quick but thorough stir, since the flour has a tendency to settle at the bottom of the jug while it rests in the fridge (especially in the gluten-free batter).

Open up the air fryer and carefully fill each pan halfway with the batter (around one-eighth of the batter in each), then quickly top each pan with 1 teaspoon of the *hellimli* topping (if using). Close the air fryer, set the temperature to 375°F (190°C) and cook for 25 minutes. Once cooked, take the Yorkshire puddings straight out of the individual pans and place onto a cooling rack, then repeat the process with the remaining batter to make eight Yorkshire puddings in total.

Taze Fasulye Yahni GREEN BEAN STEW

QUICK PREP, SLOW COOK

SERVES 6
Prep: 5–10 minutes
Cook: 4–8 hours
—

- **1 vegetable stock cube,** crumbled
- **1¼ cups (300 ml) boiling hot water**
- **3 tbsp olive oil**
- **1 large yellow onion,** peeled and roughly chopped into ½–¾ in (1–2 cm) pieces
- **3 large carrots,** peeled and sliced into ½ in (1 cm) discs
- **2 celery sticks,** roughly sliced, ½ in (1 cm) thick
- **1 lb 2 oz (500 g) Yukon Gold or Russet potatoes,** peeled and cut into 1¼ in (3 cm) chunks
- **4 garlic cloves,** finely chopped
- **1 tbsp tomato paste**
- **2 tbsp *tatlı biber salçası* (Turkish sweet/mild red pepper paste)**
- **½ tsp ground cumin**
- **1 lb 2 oz (500 g) frozen green beans**
- **1 x 14 oz (400 g) can finely chopped tomatoes**
- **½ tsp sea salt flakes** (salt to taste, depending on how salty your stock is)
- **½ tsp coarse black pepper**
- **2 bay leaves**

In a jug, whisk the crumbled stock cube into the boiling hot water until fully dissolved, and leave to one side.

Add the olive oil to a large pot and place over medium heat. Once the oil is hot, add the onion, carrots, celery and potatoes to the pot and cook for 5–6 minutes, stirring occasionally, until the edges brown and the onion starts to soften.

Add the garlic to the vegetables, stir, then add the tomato paste, *tatlı biber salçası* and cumin, and, stirring continuously, cook the spicy paste down for a couple of minutes until it releases its aroma.

Add the green beans to the pot and stir until they are fully coated in the spicy paste. Pour in the chopped tomatoes, stir and let them bubble and reduce down for 3–4 minutes.

Fill up the empty tomato can with cold water and top the jug of stock up with enough water to bring the liquid measure up to 2 cups (500 ml).

Transfer everything from the pot to your slow cooker. Season the beans and vegetables with the salt and black pepper, pour in the stock, throw in the bay leaves, cover and cook on high for 3–4 hours, or on low for 6–8 hours, until the carrots and potatoes have softened, the beans are tender and the sauce has thickened. Remove the bay leaves before serving.

Kıymalı Bezelye PEA & GROUND LAMB STEW

QUICK PREP, SLOW COOK

SERVES 4–6
Prep: 10 minutes
Cook: 4–8 hours
—

1 chicken stock cube, crumbled
2 cups (500 ml) boiling
   hot water
3 tbsp olive oil
1 large yellow onion,
   peeled and finely chopped
2 large carrots, peeled and sliced
   into ½ in (1 cm) rounds
4 medium Yukon Gold or
   Russet potatoes, peeled
   and chopped into 1¼ in
   (3 cm) chunks
1 lb 2 oz (500 g) ground lamb
1 tsp sea salt flakes
1 tsp coarse black pepper
4 garlic cloves, crushed
   or very finely grated
1 tsp paprika
¼ tsp ground cinnamon
½ tsp ground cumin
5 cups (700 g) frozen peas
1 x 14 oz (400 g) can chopped
   tomatoes
2 tbsp tatlı biber salçası
   (Turkish sweet/mild
   red pepper paste)
1 bay leaf

In a jug, whisk the crumbled stock cube into the boiling water until fully dissolved, and leave to one side.

Place the olive oil in a large pot on the stovetop over medium heat. Once the oil is hot, add the onion, carrots and potatoes to the cook down the vegetables for 10–12 minutes, until the onion starts to soften and the carrots and potatoes brown along the edges, stirring often.

Add the ground lamb to the pan, breaking it up into the vegetables with the back of a wooden spoon. Season the meat with the salt and black pepper, and cook for 5–6 minutes until browned, stirring often.

Add the garlic, paprika, cinnamon and cumin to the pan, and stir for a minute or two until the spices release their aroma.

Transfer everything from the pan into the slow cooker.

Add the frozen peas to the slow cooker, stir well, then add the chopped tomatoes, *tatlı biber salçası*, the stock and bay leaf and stir well again.

Cover and cook on high for 3–4 hours or on low for 6–8 hours until the carrots and potatoes have softened, the meat is tender and the sauce has thickened.

Remove the bay leaf. Serve with rice (or fresh bread, page 191), and thick plain yogurt.

Slow-Cooked *Bolonez*

QUICK PREP, SLOW COOK

SERVES 12 (GENEROUSLY)
Prep: 30 minutes
Cook: 6–12 hours
——

1 beef stock cube, crumbled
Scant 1 cup (200 ml) boiling hot water
4 tbsp olive oil
2 large onions, very finely chopped
4 carrots, peeled and very finely chopped
2–3 celery sticks, very finely chopped
1 tsp sea salt flakes
6 large garlic cloves, finely grated/chopped
2 lbs 4 oz (1 kg) ground beef
3 tbsp *tatlı biber salçası* (Turkish sweet/mild red pepper paste)
10½ oz (300 g) chestnut/ cremini mushrooms, very finely diced/chopped
¾ tsp coarse black pepper
2 tsp dried oregano
Scant 1 cup (200 ml) red wine
1 tbsp pomegranate molasses
1 tbsp balsamic vinegar
1 x 1 lb 9 oz (690 g) jar passata
1 x 14 oz (400 g) can finely chopped tomatoes
Scant ½ cup (100 ml) milk
2 bay leaves
A few sprigs of fresh thyme
1 large cinnamon stick

In a jug, whisk the crumbled stock cube into the boiling water until fully dissolved, and leave to one side.

Place the olive oil in a large pan and place on the stovetop over low-medium heat.

Add the onions, carrots and celery to the pan, sprinkle in half of the sea salt and allow the vegetables to soften and caramelize for 15–20 minutes, stirring occasionally.

Add the garlic and ground beef to the pan, turn up the heat and, using the back of a wooden spoon, break the meat up in the pan. After 5–6 minutes, the meat should have browned all over, so add the *tatlı biber salçası* and mix it fully into the meat. Then add the mushrooms, keeping the heat up high so that they cook quickly into the meat and vegetables. Season with the remaining salt and the black pepper and oregano.

Add the red wine, and let it reduce and bubble vigorously for a few minutes until it cooks down fully into the meat.

Carefully transfer the contents of the pan to the slow cooker.

Add the pomegranate molasses, balsamic vinegar, passata, chopped tomatoes and milk to the slow cooker and stir well. Fill up the empty tomato can and passata bottle with a little cold water, swish the water around, then pour the water from both the can and the bottle into the jug of stock to bring the liquid up to about 2 cups (500 ml).

Pour the stock into the slow cooker, add the bay leaves, sprigs of thyme and the cinnamon stick, stir well, then put the lid on and cook on high for 6–8 hours, or on low for 10–12 hours. Remove the bay leaves before serving.

Delicious Beef Short Ribs

QUICK PREP, SLOW COOK

SERVES 4–6
Prep: 15–20 minutes
Cook: 6–12 hours
—

1 beef stock cube, crumbled
2 tbsp *tatlı biber salçası*
   (Turkish sweet/mild
   red pepper paste)
2 tbsp beef gravy granules
2 tbsp pomegranate molasses
1 tbsp Worcestershire sauce
3 cups (750 ml) boiling
   hot water
6 large beef short ribs
   (around 1 lb 2 oz/500 g each)
1 tsp sea salt flakes
3 tbsp olive oil
1 tsp coarse black pepper
2 large onions, peeled and
   finely chopped
2 large carrots, peeled and
   roughly chopped
2 large celery sticks,
   roughly choppped
6 garlic cloves, peeled
   and left whole
A few sprigs of fresh rosemary
A few sprigs of fresh thyme
2 bay leaves

In a jug, whisk the crumbled stock cube, the *tatlı biber salçası*, gravy granules, pomegranate molasses and Worcestershire sauce into the boiling water until fully dissolved and smooth. Set to one side.

Season the short ribs with the sea salt. Heat 1 tablespoon of the olive oil in a large sauté pan on the stovetop over medium heat, then sear the well-seasoned short ribs, two at a time, until browned all over. Once browned, put them into your slow cooker, seasoning with the black pepper.

The short ribs can release a lot of excess fat while they're cooking, so if the oil in the pan looks like it needs replacing, carefully discard it (not down the sink), then wait for the pan to cool down for a couple of minutes, then give it a quick wipe or wash, ready to re-use.

In the pan you used to sear the ribs, add the remaining olive oil, and place over medium heat. Once hot, add the onions to the pan and soften for 4–5 minutes before adding in the carrots, celery, garlic cloves, sprigs of rosemary and thyme and the bay leaves. Once the garlic and herbs start to release their aroma, after a minute or so, pour in the stock mixture from earlier and let it come up to a boil, then take off the heat.

Pour the sauce over the ribs in the slow cooker. Place the lid on the slow cooker and cook on high for 7–8 hours, or on low for 10–12 hours. Check the short ribs a couple of hours before the cooking time is up. Once they are ready, the meat should be fully tender and falling off the bone.

Transfer the short ribs to a plate, cover them tightly in foil, then discard the bay leaves and herb stalks, and strain the sauce from the slow cooker dish into a large jug. Separate and discard the fat from the top of the sauce.

If the sauce needs thickening at this point, transfer it to a pan, place over high heat on the stovetop and keep it boiling until it thickens and reduces by about a third and you have a gravy.

Spoon the gravy over the short ribs and serve with the Baked Garlicky Parmesan & Sesame Mash (page 162) and some steamed green vegetables.

Shopping for Flavor

Here is a comprehensive list of most of the ingredients I buy each week (choosing vegetables as and when they are in season). These are my flavor essentials—building layers of deliciousness quickly and easily every single time I use them.

I have these ingredients stored in my fridge, freezer and pantry, and you'll spot them consistently appearing throughout the recipes in this book. You will also find more in-depth descriptions of a handful of typical (Turkish) Cypriot ingredients at the front of the book (pages 15–21) that might perhaps need sourcing from international or Turkish supermarkets.

Vegetables & Fruit
Avocados
Carrots
Cauliflower
Cavolo nero
Celery
Cucumber
Eggplants
Garlic
Ginger
Green beans
Kapya biber (capia pepper), red
   romano, small red bell pepper
Lemons
Mushrooms
Potatoes
Red cabbage
Red onions
Romaine/baby gem lettuce
Savoy cabbage
Scallions
Spinach
Sugar snap peas/snow peas
Sweetheart cabbage
Tomatoes
White cabbage
Yellow onions
Zucchini

Fresh Herbs
Basil
Bay leaves
Cilantro
Dill
Mint
Parsley (flat leaf)
Rosemary
Thyme

Dairy
Beyaz Peynir (Turkish white cheese)
   (see note on page 20)
Butter, unsalted
Eggs
Hellim (halloumi cheese)
Milk
Parmesan/Grana Padano cheese
Yogurt, thick plain

Other
Pickled peppers
Puff pastry
Yufka (filo pastry)

Freezer
Breadcrumbs (fresh)
Cherries
Green beans
Peas
Shrimp
Spinach

Pastas, pulses, grains & canned vegetables
Basmati rice
Black olives, dry
Brown rice (dried and pre-cooked)
Bulgur (cracked wheat), coarse
Butter beans (jarred and canned)
Cannellini beans (jarred and canned)
Chickpeas (dried, jarred and canned)
Chopped tomatoes
Durum wheat vermicelli
Green lentils (dried and canned)
Green olives, queen
Kalamata olives
Linguine

Long-grain white rice
Mini pasta shapes (anelli/ditaloni/
    ditali/macaroni)
Orzo
Parboiled long-grain rice
Quinoa (dried and pre-cooked)
Red lentils (dried)
Rice vermicelli
Short-grain white rice
Soba noodles
Spaghetti

Condiments, pastes & sauces
Anchovies
Beef stock cubes
Capers
Chicken stock cubes
Coconut milk
Dark soy sauce
Dijon mustard
Extra virgin olive oil (see note on page 15)
Honey (runny)
Instant gravy granules
Olive oil (see note on page 15)
Pickles
Pomegranate molasses (see note on page 16)
Red wine vinegar
Rice bran oil
Sunflower oil
Tahini
Tatlı biber salçası (Turkish sweet/mild
    red pepper paste—see note on page 16)
Tomato paste
Tuna
Vegetable stock cubes
White wine vinegar
Wholegrain mustard
Worcestershire sauce

Spices and dried herbs
Black pepper, coarse
Black pepper, ground
Black peppercorns
Cinnamon, stick/quill
Cinnamon, ground
Coriander, ground
Coriander seeds
Cumin, ground
Garlic granules/powder
Mint, dried
Onion granules
Oregano, dried
Paprika
Pul biber (Aleppo pepper/Turkish red
    pepper flakes—see note on page 15)
Pumpkin pie spice, ground
Sea salt, fine
Sea salt, flakes
Smoked paprika

Nuts & Seeds
Aniseed
Almonds, blanched
Almonds, ground
Almonds, sliced
Almonds, whole
Nigella seeds
Pine nuts
Pistachios
Pumpkin seeds
Sesame seeds
Sunflower seeds
Walnuts

Baking
All-purpose flour
Baking powder
Confectioners' sugar
Cornstarch
Golden syrup
Orange blossom water
Self-rising flour
Strong white bread flour
Sugar, granulated/superfine
Vanilla extract/pods
Yeast, instant/dry-active
Xanthan gum

What Recipe When?

QUICK PREP, SLOW COOK

TRADITIONAL RECIPE, CHEATER'S VERSION

TRADITIONAL FLAVORS, NEW RECIPE

Index

Acknowledgments

Dinner Tonight is full of the exciting flavors, nostalgia and sentiments that urged me to take a leap of faith to start my recipe blog in 2012, and I want to thank everyone who has had a genuine part to play in it.

It was in November 2019 that my wonderful literary agent, Juliet Pickering, contacted me to "have a chat" about my work, my ideas, and if I'd ever thought about publishing a book. Juliet, I am indebted to you; for your belief in me from the get-go, for your considered and measured manner, and the simple fact that I can pick up the phone to you whenever I want. I am thankful for your experience and your friendship, and I feel extremely lucky to have had your support for the past few years—thank you.

To my wonderful team at Ebury; Laura Higginson, Lucinda Humphrey, Alice King, Lucy Brown, Mia Oakley and Steph Reynolds, who collectively make what can often feel like a rather solitary process, very much a team effort.

Laura, I am so grateful to you for commissioning both of my cookbooks; although we didn't get to complete the journey together on *Meliz's Kitchen* (for very special reasons), it has been such a joy working with you on this one. From the initial proposal stages to where we ended up with *Dinner Tonight*, you listened and applied my vision, and my voice, intently, and I am absolutely thrilled with the beautiful book we have created. Lucie, thank you for being so patient with me, for trawling through and editing my gobbledegook, and keeping me organized throughout it all. Alice King and Mia, I have loved working with you again and am always so happy when you cook my recipes; the best kind of publicity and social content right there! Thank you, also, to Charlotte Macdonald for the taxing job of copy editing through a mountain of words (including many Turkish ones)!

Tamara Vos, what an utter pleasure it was to watch your food styling precision and flair in practice; I can't thank you enough for considerately taking the time to make my food look more beautiful than I could have imagined. Emma Cantlay, you are so talented, and so thoughtful with every little detail in my recipes, thank you. Watching you both cross recipes off the lists that were stuck to the fridge and cupboard doors gave me just as much satisfaction as it did you! #HundyP

Thank you to Luke Albert for the striking photography. Luke, you brought my recipes to life, with colors that pop and photos that magnificently jump out from the pages—I couldn't have wished for a more beautiful catalogue of my recipes.

Charlie Phillips; thank you for curating such a considerate selection of props, intertwined with my own, to create a real sense of "home."

Emma & Alex Smith from Smith & Gilmour; thank you so much for your romantic, yet bold design—I simply love how you brought the essence of our very first conversation straight into the book; warm tones and clear layouts that represent me, how I cook, and my heritage.

I'd like to thank Interlink Books for publishing my second book in the US. I feel honored to have been given the opportunity to share my stories and recipes with American audiences again.

I also need to thank the people that know me inside out. I love cooking for the people I love, and I fully appreciate (perhaps with the occasional dent to my ego) the honest feedback I receive from the straight talkers dearest to me! And so, this is for you, my lovely friends and family; you have all tried and tested the recipes in *Dinner Tonight*, have been sincere and subjective throughout the journey, and some of you have even cooked or shared recipes with me that can be found in here—thank you for the "Hodge-Podge", Sarah, for the *Kıymalı Bezelye* inspiration, Revza Abla, and for introducing me to salt beef, Elyse.

To my lovely mother-in-law Edwina: thank you for the inspiration for the sausage ragout recipe that always brings a smile to your grandchildren's faces, and to you and Barry for always encouraging my efforts. I am so lucky to have you both.

Anne (mom) and *Baba* (dad). It goes without saying that nothing I do is ever without your undivided support, willing me to reach for the things I love doing the most, for the opportunities you didn't have or were afraid to take yourselves. You have taught me to appreciate everything and everyone around me, with no judgment, and that goes for the food I have grown up cooking and putting on my own dinner table. Mum, you know I cook the way I do because of you. Thank you— I love you both so much.

Finally, I want to thank my very special ones. R & A, thank you for having a sincere interest in what mommy does, and not just because you love eating my food! When you're not asking me to make pancakes at the crack of dawn on a Saturday, you're rummaging through the cupboards to make up your own recipes. I am so thankful that you have grown up appreciating how bringing the wholesome food that we've cooked with our own hands to the table, brings joy and comfort into our lives. I love you both so very much.

Joel. Firstly, I want to apologize for writing another cookbook! A process I adore so much, and get rather lost in, that you lose me for a while, too! You are my absolute rock. Thank you for your pure, unassuming nature and patience. You are always there with your precious words of encouragement to give me confidence, honesty and support, proudly championing what I do in every breath—your love is unrivaled, and I am so incredibly grateful to have it. I love you so much.

Meliz x

First published in 2024 by

Interlink Books
An imprint of Interlink Publishing Group, Inc.
46 Crosby Street
Northampton, Massachusetts 01060
www.interlinkbooks.com

Published simultaneously in the United Kingdom by Ebury Press, an imprint of Ebury
Publishing, part of the Penguin Random House group of companies.

Copyright © Meliz Berg 2024
Photography by Luke J Albert

Library of Congress Cataloging-in-Publication Data available
ISBN 978-1-62371-689-9

Design: Smith & Gilmour
Photography: Luke J Albert
Food Styling: Tamara Vos
Prop Styling: Charlie Phillips

Color origination by Altaimage Ltd, London
Printed and bound in China by C&C Offset Printing Co., Ltd

10 9 8 7 6 5 4 3 2 1

Please visit www.interlinkbooks.com to browse
our complete catalog.